Hieroglyphs of Another World

Hieroglyphs
of Another
World

On Poetry, Swedenborg, and Other Matters

Ilya Kutik

EDITED BY ANDREW WACHTEL

NORTHWESTERN UNIVERSITY PRESS
EVANSTON, ILLINOIS

Northwestern University Press
Evanston, Illinois 60208-4210

Copyright © 2000 by Northwestern University Press.
Published 2000. All rights reserved.

Printed in the United States of America

ISBN 0-8101-1777-0

Library of Congress Cataloging-in-Publication Data

Kutik, Ilía
    Hieroglyphs of another world : on poetry, Swedenborg, and
other matters / Ilya Kutik ; edited by Andrew Wachtel.
        p. cm.
    ISBN 0-8101-1777-0
    I. Wachtel, Andrew. II. Title.
PG3482.8.U76H54 2000
891.74'5—dc21

                                            00-008148

CONTENTS

Acknowledgments / vii

Introduction: Smoke, or Notes from the Book / ix

PART I
On Poetry

Odysseus's Bow / 5

The Tormentor of Life / 10

The Short Course of the RCP
Recent Catacomb Poetry / 23

After the Future / 31

Swedish Dialogue on Poetry / 36

On Reading Aigi / 46

Invitation to the Sentimental / 53

PART II
On Swedenborg and Other Matters

Verlaine's Violin / 63

Longer than a Line, or
The "Correspondences" of Hans Viksten / 67

Hieroglyphs of Swedish Poetry / 81

Stagnelius's Mustache / 87

From the Book *Accidents,
Coincidences, and Correspondences* / 105

The Poet of Flowers: Linnaeus / 105
The Poetry of Money / 107
The Poetry of Trolls / 110
Solitaire of Coincidences: Balthus and Kevin / 112
Gustav III / 116

Twelve Stories about Swedenborg / 119

ACKNOWLEDGMENTS

First and foremost, I want to thank the "staff" that was "employed" in order to make this book possible in English: the editor (Andrew Wachtel) and the translators (the editor, Michael Denner, Michael Hazin, Lyn Hejinian, Peter Thomas, and Justin Weir). Second, many of these essays wouldn't be written if not for direct commissions from various journals, magazines, and newspapers from all over the world, mostly from Scandinavia (*Aftonbladet* and *Artes,* Sweden) and Germany (*Frankfurter Rundschau*). My thanks go to the editors over there. Third, the Swedenborg part of this thin volume is very much indebted to what remains to this day the best biography of this great man: *The Swedenborg Epic* by Cyriel Odhner Sigstedt. There, he is a *person*. Here, he is a *persona*, a *personage*. Hence, all my "displacements," "mistakes," and "inexactitudes" are on purpose. I also bow to Alia Fedoseeva and Igor Pomerantsev, both from Radio Liberty, who kept inspiring me—during my five years in Sweden—to produce numerous though short writings on topics related to it. If those were all gathered together, they could have made another volume: not "better" but definitely "fatter." And last but not least, I would like to thank my editors at Northwestern University Press, Susan Harris and Susan Betz.

INTRODUCTION
Smoke, or Notes from the Book

Another name for this book could be *One Thousand and One Cigarettes.*

First, poetry—and this book *is* on poetry and connected matters—is a kind of Delphic smoke, and, believe it or not, I am still certain of this: It provokes Pythian metaphors, which can always be read this or that way. Think, however, how many heroes were inspired by those Delphic metaphors, despite or due to their wrong—and thus right—interpretations.

Second, this book is a *narrative* "on poetry, Swedenborg, and other matters," that is, some Scheherazade's "hookah," which is supposed to hook your attention as long as possible.

Third, poetry and narratives about poetry shouldn't, to my mind, differ very much: Both ought to look like those famous smoke rings of Sir Winston Churchill, through which only Churchill was able to blow a single plume. (Readers will find another version of the same metaphor in the first essay, "Odysseus's Bow.")

And fourth, I smoked an even larger number of late-night cigarettes in the course of the approximately ten years during which I produced this volume. Although I don't want to look—at least in the very beginning—like a total egomaniac, I cherish with pleasure the great observation by Louis MacNeice about Auden: "Everything he touches turns to cigarettes." Moreover, when going through Richard Beard's *X20: A Novel of (Not) Smoking,* a metaphysical kind of fiction dedicated to our common addiction and to our (not) giving it up, I—still a smoker—immediately scented a cute phrase, "If you took up writing to give up smoking, how are you going to give up writing?" What can I say?

Well, "But what is behind all these Londonesque fogs of yours?" would be, apparently, one's question. There are two sections connected by the stream (plume) of my life—without a capital *L*—which got me first from Moscow to Sweden and then to the United States.

Being a Russian, I haven't even touched—although my compatriots used to read almost everything—the only Russian novel called directly *Smoke*. Its author is our nineteenth-century classic, Ivan Turgenev. While thinking these introductory notes over, however, I somehow realized that I should at least scan it—to test whether my bias about it—that is, my intuition—was correct; and, yes, the novel, I discovered, was about Turgenev's life *disappointments*—in both Russia and Western Europe. In the latter, he first traveled from time to time and then resided permanently.

Still, I am writing all this not because I live now in emigration (like, say, Turgenev), or because I am interested in the metaphysics of *smoke* (though I truly am and often refer to it in this book; see, for example, the "Swedenborg" second section, in which I call it *mist*), or in order to emphasize that as an American literature professor I now push myself into reading even trashy stuff—of which this novel of Turgenev, unfortunately, is a part—just to know what it says. Not at all. I simply want to state that this collection of mine is not about *any* disappointments, period. On the contrary, it is about my high *appreciation* of both my native Russia and my adopted West. It is "about" how I feel and thus *participate* in the "cultural differences" of both. Moreover, those two turned into a kind of personal solitaire, and you'll find pages and pages, semitheoretical or more entertaining, dedicated to this concept (I call it "a rhyme of Fate"—see, for example, "The Tormentor of Life"). Even the cover, about which I have thought a lot, attempts to summarize two parts of this book: "theoretical" (first) and "entertaining" (second). On the cover—after Natalia Goncharova—World War I airplanes cross their wings with an angel's, and that is exactly how I understand the teamwork of both parts of this work. (Strictly speaking, readers will discover some "on angels" pages, too.)

And now, perhaps, my final smoke ring. This book, I hope, maintains the Russian poetic essayistic tradition, even despite the fact that two essays in it, including this preface, were written in English. What I mean by this Russianness is merely the essay's external and internal formalities: Their parts look separate, and the author is very jumpy—he doesn't provide readers with the "bridges" between them; however, the bridges exist, and one just has to figure them out, leaning on his or her *associational* endowment. In short, the reader—in order to make many ends (metaphors, puns, associations) meet—has to make a whole from what just *looks* separate and will thus finally get a finished jigsaw puzzle. (Also, see the essay "After the Future.")

I call it a Russian poetic essayistic tradition, though I can name here a few contemporary American authors who are somehow very close to a similar style: Mark Strand, Charles Simic, and Guy Davenport, for example. This is not even to speak of the great Russian poet Joseph Brodsky, who wrote most of his many essays in his adopted English and to whom I am personally deeply indebted.

Yes, my plume is almost over now. It should, probably, have been dedicated to a very young friend of mine, Samuel Barnes W., who believes that my real smoke rings make me a kind of Tolkien wizard. I perform them for him each time he politely asks. Though I am not a wizard, his young faith makes me feel stronger and even suggests—in the case of this collection—that it won't necessarily vanish into thin air. Oxymorons happen.

Ilya Kutik
Evanston, 1999

Hieroglyphs of Another World

PART I

On Poetry

Like golden knights of numbers, we rule at tables round.
—Ilya Kutik, "Hour's Wasp"

Odysseus's Bow

1

Somewhere, although I'm not sure that this is right, I read that a poetic text as a whole is a necklace from which the string was pulled out, and the pearls (we'll call them pearls) remained in place.

For me, the creative process (as in meaning and "duration") is that place in *The Odyssey* which describes the competition among the suitors: stringing Odysseus's bow, warming up the bowstring, rubbing it with fat, and, before that, a sacrifice (otherwise, where would the fat have come from? . . .). And then, all at once, His appearance. He comes up, hunched and in tatters, his calves beset with cramps—a goddess's anesthetic; but then he straightens up from under the ether, thunder (a sign from heaven), on his cheekbones and muscles the tattoo of "rosy-fingered" strength; he concentrates, and the bow bends! The arrow passes through the rings in all twelve ax heads that had been placed into the earth. It touches none of them and flies straight to the target. There you have creation, an act. O Penelope!

And for me, *that* is a poem. It is that arrow from Odysseus's bow which passes untouched through all the parts (each strophe is a ring) and hits the target.

2

This stringlet of ring-shaped meanings is like a metaphysical thread. And in its path the arrow pulls that thread, which gradually melts into the "sky" of the subconscious, in the same way that the vapor trail of a jetliner becomes invisible as the arrow flight hurtles forward.

3

The rings comprise *all* cultures—Hellas, Rome, Judea, Byzantium. . . . "Air" (limited by the surprised hermeticism of a "ring"), like an arrow, is taken from each of them; it's joined to the sharp air whistle of flight. Like a funnel, the flight movement pulls the air into itself and carries it away while still remaining in the same place. The deflowering of an absent hymen.

An example (the best one) is the eight-line strophe of Mandelstam. An attempt (a personal one) is my "Ode on Visiting the Belosaraisk Spit on the Sea of Azov."*

This (in the ode and in general) is, for me, a solution to the problem of the Whole, of nostalgia in an epic key.

4

Poetry as a Game.

My pseudo-intellectualism (but "pseudo" with a plus sign, "in the spirit" of T. Mann, T. S. Eliot, J. L. Borges, and E. A. Poe) is the *only* way to create myth: to tell (or speak) with *such* an intonation that it all *is* and *was*. According to Pasternak, poetry is the cognition of one's own rectitude; but it would be better to say that it is

---

*For a bilingual edition of this work, see Ilya Kutik, *Ode on Visiting the Belosaraisk Spit on the Sea of Azov*, translated by Kit Robinson (New York: Alef, 1995).

creation! From romanticism, we know that an utterance is irreversible. That's why Mandelstam said that poetry is power.

5

With his poetics, Aristotle arrested all of old European culture.

With the loss of "norms and rules," the postfolkloric epoch of the Whole as such disappeared forever.

6

Neoclassicism was the last attempt to resurrect—to create—the Whole at the cost of the loss of the depth of images. I translated Alexander Pope's "Essay on Man" into Russian. He writes:

> What's fame? a fancied life in other's breath,
> A thing beyond us ev'n before our death. . . .
>
> (Fourth Epistle)

But he should have said:

> What's fame? a wind we only know about
> from curtains that come billowing out.

In the first instance (Pope's), there is only an utterance. In the second, there's an utterance and an image simultaneously. As a "fragment," the first gives no more information than it contains, while the second *already* behaves as a Whole, even with nothing else. Pope is the *pointillist* of the eighteenth century—he creates his Whole out of aphoristic point utterances. But that is *not* flight but knitting.

7

A yearning for the epoch of the Whole can be felt in the epic tones of Shelley's "Ozymandias": in the desert, bits and pieces of something—arms? legs?—and the echo of the Whole is the Voice. Do we reader-Stanislavskians believe him? Yes, a cold breath, like an arrow, forces

its way through the air; but the quivering of its tail feathers, like the
skeleton of an extinct animal, leaves an impression in stone.

8

Does that mean that something whole (that is, wholer by itself) is
already a residue (a fragment as a "loudspeaker" of the whole) if
the *entire* strength of what is missing is hidden in it? . . . The part is
greater than the Whole. A principle of the baroque? Yes. Or, per-
haps, it is classicism from the point of view of a paleontologist for
whom the skeleton of a dinosaur is more important and meaning-
ful than the "monster" itself?

What has remained of, say, the *Annals* of Ennius? Lines, a few
verses, and parts of verses . . . , but *that* is the same as the "result-
residue" of all "anthology poets," outsiders to *that* culture (to use a
contemporary term). The lesser have turned out to be equal to the
greater. It's almost a Borges poem.

9

The *whole* must be such that *each* of its *fragments* is *self-sufficient*,
but when taken together they form a kind of metaphysical *unity*.
That is my principle.

10

According to Shpet, poetry is strength + turning. Aigi interprets it
to mean the ability at any speed ("strength") to control the wheel (to
write yourself into your turns). But this is just a "game" with the
Whole. Rocks or splashes (lines) fly off the tires. And what will you
do with them?

11

I write "Jesus whose piscine scales. . . ." There's a line. Without any
continuation. Poetry's a desert of sounds, but it's not every one that
engenders a whirlwind.

Sosnora, who is deaf, was told that in the United States he could have an operation after which he would be able to hear everything but only in a continuous way—that is, without being able to differentiate separate sounds.

The poet hunts for sounds from just this kind of "chaos," in strophes and lines, and only later does he "write in" everything that fills the space between them. For example, I hear the following:

> . . . . Litti's madonna
> . . . .
> . . . . . . like a person who's on Soma
> with eyes more still than stillness, and
> . . . .

And then, for example, between the first and second line I could insert "under Leonardo's hand" or something like that. The profession is the unavoidable "profanation" of space. The beginning of "craft."

12

I believe, yes, I believe that Faulkner (was it only he?) hung pieces of paper with a most detailed list of the events of each hour/day/ chapter of his latest novel on the walls.

For me, the poetic text is movement from strophe to strophe, "hung" in the subconscious and conscious mind, from sound to sound.

But the principle of collage, of montage, is outdated: from Shershenevich (poetry) and Eisenstein (film) to Rauschenberg (painting).

What remains is the principle of the "fragment," "the craft," of Odysseus's arrow. Or, as Pasternak says:

> The game and torture
> Of achieved triumph
> Is the drawn bowstring
> Of a taut bow.

But I'm not sure that I won't "renounce" this principle. For if something is "achieved," then *what* is Penelope for?

Translated by Andrew Wachtel

The Tormentor of Life

for André Markovicz

Creativity

"I *think,* therefore I am." The sounding board of this Cartesian aphorism resonates so loudly that it may snap the instrument's strings. And where is he, that Paganini, that black tomcat with diamond eyes, who might "teach" even one string "to sing"?

The *paradox* (the small change of philosophy before Hegel and of Hegelian philosophy as well)—is it more convertible than the ruble? Of course, when I eat (in Russian, *ia em*), I am. But when I reason, "think," I am *not* in that circle where people eat, drink, love, walk—that is, where they exist. When I think, I find myself in a world (of thoughts) which has nothing to do with *this* one: I try to step in, to join the round dance of these thoughts, to grab one hand and take another, but I am not *here,* since I don't *feel* this world.

My blood, even without me, will lead *its* own, always wintry, pagan round dance inside me, and still the dance circles my heart, circles that crackling bonfire of my pledge and promises, to keep my body warm. But a paradox, alas, very quickly burns out.

The ability to "think," to imagine, to create, is precisely the barrier between me and normal, "commonly experienced" existence: between existence and essence. I deprive myself of a part of *this* life, for the sake of *that* one, but it's *not* a matter of choice—it's an inevitability. The romantics made a tragedy of this, viewing it as the "sacrifice" which elevates them *above* those they leave behind. I view it simply as an inevitability and only that, entailing all the "inconveniences" in *this* life connected with it. And indeed, not inconveniences but torments.

Creativity is *the tormentor of life.*

Metaphor

A paradox, of course, is a unit measuring complexity, when for every "yes" there is a "no" (and not only one) and vice versa. Rozanov felt this very strongly; he could write an article one day on, say, what a genius Pushkin was, and the next day he might describe him as something quite the opposite; but one thing and then the other are not self-contradicting truths. There is a lot of this in Pavel Florensky's works as well.

But the point is that the paradox connecting these "oppositions" with each other, these yeses and nos, is easily "refuted" by some other paradox, and what remains, as a result, is no more than an interesting, "funny" *thought.*

The only "unit of complexity" which cannot be "refuted" is the *metaphor.* It combines within itself any yeses and nos; it is the only convincing certificate of their marriage, sanctified by artistic merit. There are no others.

Rhythm

The world where poets exist is a world of rhythm not chosen by them. Everything, including language, begins from the rhythm in the poet. That thing called inspiration only pushes the "power" button, like that on a radio, and turns the tuning dial until a flashing signal appears somewhere within to indicate that the wave vibrations of the invisible antenna have matched up with the receiving unit.

Properly speaking, the "mysterious" element in all this is the "switching on" instant, which can occur as something completely unexpected among the parallel and dissonancing rhythms of *this* life, or it can result as the consequence of a long entry into meditation. Moreover, this translation already bears the exactness of an Image within itself, but only in its rhythmic form.

Meter

Meter is the earthly adequacy of *that* rhythm.

Meter for the poet is the same as notes for a composer, that is, a method for receiving and transmitting sounds by means of an algebraic "limitation."

Often, meter cringes before rhythm like a caterpillar whose gait involves both creeping and curves; it almost draws a "diagram" of the iamb:

> . . . or we close ourselves *off from* ourselves as this *worm turns* into a hook and then a handle . . .

More rarely, it's a butterfly, breaking out of its maddening cocoon and flexing in the air like a tennis player—ball to the ground: boom-boom, bounce-stroke-bounce-stroke. The more agitated the butterfly, the more its plane vibrates over the surface, the longer and more irregular the pause between each stroke and bounce will be.

Rhyme

Rhyme is the logical extension of rhythm and its "basis."

Meter, as the record of rhyme, that is, of the sound vibration of the Image, divides sound, like Plato's androgyne, into male and female halves eternally striving to unite. The attempt to unite and the impossibility of doing so produce rhyme, and very frequently an Image appears through it.

Indeed, for me, a rhyme is like two terminals whose connection provides current to the Image and "forms" its field.

Poetics

Having spoken of rhyme, meter, and so forth, however, I've suddenly remembered that all this is what is known as poetics. As for me, this word must immediately—on being uttered—be stopped by asterisks. Discussions of it are boring and sentimental. It's like kissing a mirror.

The stink of grease rises off it as from a dismantled motor. It is far more interesting to talk about motion than about whatever "prompts" it.

I rhyme not because—or not *only* because—I want it *that* way, but also because, as I deeply believe, *everything* in the world is rhymed. And has been since long before the appearance of poetry. It only makes what's concealed manifest, true—or it tries to do so.

One cannot escape rhyme any more than Fate. Here lies its metaphysical "suspense." Here is an example: Esenin's noose, already open, tightened in the form of a scarf around Isadora Duncan's neck. Both were strangled. Suicide and bad luck. But there's no more "luck" here than in a rhymed couplet.

It is rhyme that is truly regular in its unexpectedness, and this is no paradox but a law, one which, every time it is revealed, is frightening and interesting all over again.

For this reason, free verse very often seems to be a form of escapism to me, an attempt to run away, to hide from Fate, which all the same will rhyme. And it is "successful" only in those cases where such a flight is envisaged, as it were, beforehand, by Fate itself, and is bound by its "meter" and "rhythm."

I rhyme because I'm a fatalist. I sense angels at my elbows; I don't feel the need to use them to push through the crowd of words and assonances. For me, this crowd is no less corporeal than a real crowd. The crowd might block the way, but unless such a thing is *fated*, it won't happen: The members of the crowd will lead and accompany me. . . . I repeat that I'm a fatalist.

I believe in rhyme as Pythagoras believed in number. And as he who, according to legend, remembered his four incarnations; I recall the line from *Marburg*—"and everything was in his likeness"—which certainly was written not only *before* Boris Pasternak but also B.C.

I believe in the Word, that is, in God. The direct interdependence of destiny and character is obvious for me even acoustically.

To my Russian ear, for example, all Byronism and all the sources of romantic *arrogance* (in Russian, *gordynya*) are in the name "Gordon." And "lord" sounds like *gord*. A name, as a person's very first word, has a strange power over the psyche and therefore over a person's deeds and destiny. Whence comes, for example,

John Donne's famous "for whom the bell tolls? It tolls for thee," if not from his own name, which dictated to him, with its "donn-donn," not only this line but the whole of his fate as a pastor?

Like echo and ear, like Narcissus and the mirror, such is the poet and his or her "poetics."

> A stone thrown in a peaceful pond
> Will weep your own name's sound.

Thus said Tsvetaeva of Blok.

But what poetry is, I don't know. Just as dust accumulates in the creases of pockets and briefcases, so poetry accumulates in the folds of the heart, which we later turn inside out in our attempts to extract it. And what is dust? According to scientific data, it contains tiny scales of our skin, which we change scarcely less often than do snakes. Poetry . . . dust . . . changes of skin. The torment is *not* in the accumulation but in the waiting—*while* it accumulates, *until* it is heard.

Image as Form and Content

Pasternak says that art, that is, poetry, is not a fountain but a sponge.

Certainly a poet is a sponge, since what he or she does all the time is absorb.

The conciseness of Pasternak's aphorism is inversely proportionate to the immensity that the poet must "soak up" into him- or herself, so as later to wring it out, as Pasternak says, "for the glory of the paper."

But the sponge is a poet, not poetry. The latter, obviously, is beyond formulas.

Besides, the poet is an Image, a figure, which he takes on as a personality. The identity of the poet with poetry (as Pasternak put it when stating his "reservations") is a peculiarly romantic image, above all Byronic, engaged in a debate with the surf, where poems and elemental forces (in Russian, *stikhi* and *stikhiya*) form a "Siamese" rhyme, like "verb" and "verb," where the word and the part of speech signifying action have been one from inception.

It's not hard to tease a public bull with an image banderilla.

This kind of corrida was set up by Victor Hugo with his red

vest, and Maiakovsky managed it with his notorious yellow blouse, which has faded considerably in the detergents of memoirs.

For the romantics, social conduct was the pivot of their "poetics," or, rather, it forms the context of their poetry. In other words: Here he is—I—and the world is all that's "not-I," or $I > world$ (in algebraic terms); and herein lies a full-scale conflict. This is the discovery, appropriately French, of the existentialists, who were themselves romantics, and it is jauntily expressed by Sartre in his comment, "Hell is other people."

And so the life of the poet becomes the context for poetry, and this context depends entirely on the extent to which life is dramatic, on the extent to which the Colosseum and the collisions within life rhyme.

"He who has never tasted tears with his bread has never met the forces of heaven," said Goethe, in Tiutchev's words.

This isn't the whole truth, but it brings personality to a dead end. Life as context, then, must at all times "meet the standards" of the Image.

What can the contemporary romantic poet do, having been crowned with all possible laurels and having attained worldly happiness? It's better to stop writing; it's worse to commit a crime, go to prison, and write a new book inspired by biographical suffering. Verlaine wrote *Sagesse*, his best book, in prison, tortured not by his conscience but by deprivations, richly illuminated by hallucinations—not unlike Rimbaud, thanks to whom he found himself in this situation in the first place. And could it be the rhyme of Fate that the present-day French are so afraid to see on paper?

Ego and Epos

In my opinion, even delirium tremens (the phrase in Russian translates as "white fever") is more engaging and "productive" than the theme of a sufferer standing before a mirror. On the other hand, this is what is known as masochism, which seems to cut facets in the soul as if it were a stone, making the soul's magnificence more paradoxical and capricious, while at the same time making it more "predictable." The poet himself attracts it, in any case. Everything that he does, he does willy-nilly and on his own.

But "poet" is a word which is under the pressure, as it were, of its own importance. One feels uneasy near it, as if surrounded by a marble interior, the interior of a palace or a morgue. If I could, I would give it the designation *obs.* and replace it with something more flexible, like "artist" or "actor."

The actor, as a personality, suggests first of all an ability to absorb as much as possible and to squeeze out as much as possible. An actor's egoism involves pulling all possible feelings to the center of the "I." One might be impressed by Trotsky or Saint Francis of Assisi, but an artist doesn't ever become a terrorist or a monk. He is like a yogi, who can "pull" the powers of all his organs into his plexus by virtue of certain asanas.

"I" is the maximum widening of the eye and the other senses. The world > myself, but I = world, because I know this, because it exists precisely *through* me, *by* me, since *only* I see it as such and am able to "stage" it. In my view, the whole of personalism is stage direction and nothing more. Poetry without the "I-world" conflict becomes no more conformist and impersonal than Kant's axiom: "The starry sky . . ." and so on.

As I see it, creativity requires two things: solitude and a home front. The home front is "you"; the solitude is "I." Without "you," "I" feels lost, a "singularity." "Singularity" is antiartistic. It is merely existential: One experiences but doesn't express. If one is given a home front, one's solitude is a temporary, necessary distance between the constancy of a sense of the world, the world order, and freedom of sensation (self-sensation); it is in this gap that creativity is possible.

For me, the entire conflict is in seeking a way to express the light-wave figure that I sense.

My conflict is an Old Testament night battle with language; one cannot win, but one may at least refuse to surrender. And though language, like everything in the universe, grows old and decays, there is no new language. New languages could only provide a means of assimilation, the capacity to see things anew and to compare.

Language is eaten away by caries. But each era, like a dentist, sets its own epos upon it, like Dante's golden crown.

For me, this means that epos is not a genre category, like that of the epic, say, but, rather, it is ontological, even when we in our own times feel how much we are "godforsaken."

Modernism and Postmodernism

Today, there is no avant-garde. This is an era not of forging ahead but of summing up. Forging ahead creates a rupture; summing up achieves a necessary distance—like a magnet which attracts the (naturally) "attracted." The distance created is its (magnetic) field.

Postmodernism is a latter-day magnet. It bristles, hedgehoglike, resembling a magnet overgrown with nails. But a hedgehog is at harmony when it's curled up. A hedgehog is round, like an epic. An epic is always characterized by "roundness," by the round weight of a ball.

Postmodernism is already *epic*, by virtue of its gathering nature, by virtue of being *post*.

Every era "examines" the others from its point of view. "From the point of view" of postmodernism, everything else (including itself) is of almost "zoological" interest. Classicism, for example, has the proportions of a temple and an elephant whose ears are already "baroque" (the exaggeration of detail).

Modernism is an exotic beast which threateningly shows the fangs of device. Postmodernism, as I have said, is a hedgehog.

And herein lies the major difference between them: Modernism shows its devices, while postmodernism hides them, curling around them, a multitude of bristles.

Devices in modernism are personalized; they constitute *style*. Jason threw a stone into a crowd of warriors who'd sprung from dragon's teeth, and they killed each other.

Postmodernism is primordially "antipersonal": At best, its "I" is that of an observer of an astronomical equinox of styles. God confused the languages of the builders at Babel and therein rests the beginnings of geography and linguistics. Thus Viacheslav V. Ivanov seeking this Ur-language is a "postmodernist," while the surrogate Esperanto is a logical product of Babel's arrogant modernist personalism.

Here postmodernism doesn't "meddle." One of the unwritten laws of the epic states: If Achilles threw a spear, even Homer couldn't stop it.

Genre

Let's posit that the Epos is unknowable.

The ordinary tripartite mirror is a parody, as it were, of the

idea of the Holy Trinity when the mirror is opened out and espe-
cially when it is closed up. Something is rationally "explained," but
as a matter of fact. . . .

Any epic construction is just such a "tripartite mirror," since it
has a rational foundation supporting it, an axis around which ev-
erything is built. Including mythology and heroics, at one time.

Genre, in my opinion, has become just such an epic axis for
postmodernism. I say so conditionally, since it is hard to define
with scholarly precision which genre forms this axis. Genre "mists
over," like eyeglasses at the change of temperature when one goes
out into the rain from a warm room. Postmodernism, in general, is
all climates at once. It's the game of "warm and cold" played with
blindfolded eyes; genre is what has been hidden. And yet is it still
hidden somewhere? Yes, in the farthest most secret "room"—in
the artist's subconscious. It comes—quite officially within itself—
out of some generic *premise*, as conditional as the subconscious-
ness that's specifically ours.

There is another thing that's clearly important: A genre "cho-
sen" in such a way is radically devoid of eclecticism.

Eclecticism is modernist. It is this that, Jason-like, brings
styles into conflict and provokes them into battle, resulting in vic-
tory for itself.

Postmodernism is loyal; it is tolerant, within itself, of even that
which is most contradictory; it is truly "polyphonic." But this is
not the polyphony of philosophical or parliamentary debate, be-
cause a "subject" of discussion simply doesn't exist. "The starry sky
is above me, and the categorical imperative within me."

Postmodernism is free of aggression and self-defense. The op-
position between "East and West" has been eliminated; it makes
no distinction between the wrinkled face of a walnut and the wrin-
kled face of Rembrandt; it puts everything in its place as in a good
collection, and things get along and peacefully "converse," as if
they were in Paradise.

"The lion and the timid doe" ride together in one genre cart, to
paraphrase the fable.

The ode in its time was for me such a genre. Nowadays, the
cinema of Wim Wenders might serve as an example, as I wanted to
explain in an article I've never written, though these last two sec-
tions were "stolen" from it.

What and How

Having intended originally to explain how I write, I realize now that that is precisely what I can't do. What, for example, can a skier say of the reason his body at one moment tilts at a particular angle and his foot shifts suddenly at the precisely perfect instant? What can a dog say of the reason his saliva drips from its gland and of his so-called "conditioned reflex"? The monument to Pavlov's dogs in Moscow is as natural as a monument to poets. They have similar reflexes and they similarly salivate, though for poets the latter is called poetry.

Perhaps animals are even more the poets since they think exclusively in images, though they can't express them in language.

I've exhausted myself with self-analysis; I can no longer tell what is primary and what secondary. Like Brodsky's Siamese twins, "one is drinking, but both are drunk." There is always the hangover, however, to signal the awakening in one's soul of even uncommitted sins.

"What" and "how"—these are like the school assignment about the pool with two pipes, which my father always solved instead of me, and the answer to which I've completely forgotten.

Image and Likeness

I can only add that I'm completely uninterested in intruding like a bumblebee on the Kantian bud of objects and abstractions and thus pollinating the deceptive empiricist with my cross-referencing rhyme. The idea of a thing is far more interesting to me than the thing on its own; the imagination is more interesting than any natural phenomenon, even one of a more lofty order. Thus, for me, the illuminations and pyrotechnics of festivals are more interesting than the light effects called sunrise and sunset; so, too, is the make-up on a woman's face.

The world within a tree, of which I know nothing and about which I can only guess, is more interesting to me than the tree itself, about which I know everything, since I see it every day. Or, perhaps, I don't know anything, but it has *already* been created and leafed through many times by the nature that created it.

In just such a way, having looked *into* ourselves, we ascertain that all our real suffering and the darkest corners of torment can be readily found in the encyclopedia known as the literature of the world, and in its reference book, known as lyric poetry. But one has merely to gaze at these same things on the *outside*, or at one-self—the subject of experience—as an object, to feel a wave of interest such as one feels reading adventure stories.

If I could, I would write about the autonomous life of a nerve at the moment of excitation, about the general state of the eye when we see. Such a "view" I would call "epic," and probably the Creator regards us, its image and likeness, in just such a way.

Language and Speech

From the point of view of metaphor, there are the same number of horses in the "horse power" of an automobile engine as there are in a soap bubble in the bath. That is why I am looking for similarities, not for analogies. I'm not making comparisons, I'm inserting "equal signs."

Analogies are dragonfly wings, the small lenses of a scholar's pince-nez, constantly sliding off his nose and hanging from the string of "intellectual" talk over a cup of tea, obviously attracted to the flower on its porcelain.

The poetry of "speech" is the poetry of talk, the poetry of the summer house, which can be in any language, since it is subsidiary. The main thing is not to let the information spill out, but to carry it as far as the lips and stomach, to speak and feel satisfied by what has been said. In one way or another, language is always seeking to become speech, to dissolve in expression.

But—for all that—language is interesting to me for its inner autonomy, for its processes, reminiscent of the life of a cell, and biologically fascinating in just that way.

I love to contemplate language as an object which, as if by some magician's telekinesis, abruptly begins to move. There is a kind of linguistic Buddhism that poetry provokes—active or, in the words of Gadamer, "the game itself plays, drawing the players in."

Language poetry is hard to translate; each word in it is born a Word, in its image and likeness; meaning devolves from a word, through a principle resembling that which allows cells to divide and in which language is exactly the subject of speech.

I finish these excessively disparate notes in Sweden under its blue-and-yellow flag resembling the yellow-and-blue flag of Ukraine where I was born; I am astonished over and over at the *precise* rhyming of Fate.

"Oh, Best of Artists, torment but do not leave me without Your inspiration!" With such a prayer I begin every blessed day and finish these lines.

Amen.

Moscow and Lund, May 1989–July 1990

Postscript

Going through these pages as a reader, I discovered that there are some charges to be lodged against their author.

First, there's no need to tread on Hegel's hard-earned calluses; he was a genius, and in taking such a step the author is clearly immature, as he is in philosophy generally.

And here we have a divergent view of paradox, one which, despite reproof, appears on every page. And despite the author's having made the proviso (and obviously we should understand him in his own terms) that only the image (it is true that he takes this in the narrow sense, which he calls metaphor) eliminates—"with a wave of the hand"—the inner contradiction of any assertion. He is probably right about this. And he has the excuse that no essay, at least none of those I have read, has twisted the *!* out from under the exclamatory punch of the paradoxical. Genre is genre. Apparently (to return to Hegel), the author meant that no intellectual system has the capacity to settle accounts with eternity, since it doesn't know what kind of currency is in use there, and that only art won't answer questions, since in itself it is the same rhetorical question as is a stone or a tree.

Second, in calling creativity "the tormentor of life," the author would always have us understand that creativity is a life vest—as life sinks, drowning, creativity forces a displacement, pushing the body of art up to rise over every "suffering."

Third, in talking about the epic, the author is always exiling himself from the Paradise it offers through a very individualistic production of speech, which leads us to suspect the presence of that same "romantic" in him but one who hates his face in the mirror.

Fourth, even the split "I" of the "reader-writer" is proof that everything is based on a dichotomy whose scissors are always cutting the curling locks of any utterance. It's for this reason that the author is probably right that he should be writing poetry instead of fiction.

Translated by Lyn Hejinian and Michael Hazin

The Short Course of the RCP
Recent Catacomb Poetry

> It is impossible to embrace the Unembraceable.
> —K. Prutkov

1

Here's one of Pushkin's much anthologized verses. A verse-tempter. A six-foot iamb with a masculine caesura.

> On earth there is no joy,
> But there is peace, and freedom.

It has always seemed to me that this is not a poetic line at all but some sort of Berlin Wall, divided into East and West. . . .

Oh, caesura, the customhouse of verse, "Stop!" at the border of a foot: "Your passport! Is your visa in order for the second half?"

And then the second hemistich, the neon dream of those "deprived of happiness." That sly dog Alexander Pushkin! He always dreamed of breaking through the border! It didn't matter what direction, even toward the Chinese, with their feline grimaces. . . . Even then the powers that be stroked one's ego for a little while, but already they weren't letting just anyone go abroad. "On earth there is no joy. . . ."

2

". . . But there is peace, and freedom." The Soviet intelligentsia stayed a maidenly idealist with regard to the West for quite some time, and perestroika turned out to be her first lover.

The deflowering of the caesura.

Until then, she (the intelligentsia) knew of the West only from stories and books, and she read them as if in a mirror, like Leonardo's handwriting. That is, completely in reverse. If it said "bad," she read "good," because she knew "bad" firsthand, and there could be no "worse."

This mirrorlike reading produced a reversal of sides. The left (in the Western sense) became the right, and the right, the left. Without an understanding of that, it is impossible to understand recent Russian literature and even the literature of today.

By the way, they were already knocking "leftism" out of us in (Marxist or, in Western jargon, leftist) grade school, forcing even lefties to write only right-handed.

3

The caesura was the Shakespearean wet-nurse to several generations. I love our "sixties people." They "oozed out" beyond the caesura; for us they were the incarnated knowledge of ins and outs. "Great Wall of China! Great Tower of Ostankino! . . . Paths and lairs, lairs and paths," wrote my comrade Ivan Zhdanov.

The "sixties people" were in our eyes figures formed out of freezing chunks of air from the other side, Andersen's magical crystals. We marveled at their shining coats no less than their revolutionary compositions.

In the West, the "sixties people" have been misnamed "Soviet beatniks." That name isn't right, because the sides in the mirror are mixed up, as I've already said. Not without reason does the abbreviation "S.U." look like "U.S." in the mirror.

So it's nobody's fault that on the "eastern" side of the caesura we saw them as the Dante of legend, only in reverse. People would point to Dante and say, "He was in Hell." And we would say, "They were in heaven."

On the "western" side, the "sixties people" were perceived literally according to the Dante legend.

But besides Dante's *Inferno*, there is Milton's Hell, and there—a description that makes my guts "twist" from pleasure every time: Satan's black wings on the golden surface of heaven. The blind Milton probably saw as do we, whose vision is accustomed to the catacombs. . . . Khrushchev's "Thaw" was the time of their golden ascent. . . .

I recall a certain night of poetry in Ostankino, already at the very end of the Brezhnev seventies, at which contemporary poets were to read their favorite poems by another poet. One of the "sixties people," completely unexpectedly, read not Pasternak or Khlebnikov, but Blok:

> From days of war, from days of freedom
> A blood-red reflection's on everyone's face.

The "Dantesque" image of a generation . . . it sounded beautiful, even daring, and to this day I still blush from tenderness, remembering. . . . (Perestroika, by the way, was the work of "sixties people." It was their *revanche*.)

4

I am not writing criticism, but you can't get rid of history with irony. My generation all but became the "sixties people" of the eighties, and it would have, had perestroika ended earlier. . . . In any case, that's how we were perceived from both sides of the caesura. But in contrast to the "sixties people," who succeeded in "oozing through," we (under Brezhnev) came up against the caesura and tried to make the first hemistich habitable. Russian literature made of the caesura self-styled "Swedish wall bars," a gymnastic apparatus that is best for doing chin-ups.

5

One could now probably say that the caesura has favorably influenced literature. Literature pumped up its muscles, although many of them couldn't take it.

> On earth there is no joy,
> But there is peace, and freedom.
> If you're a poet, boy,
> Don't shun the booze. . . .

Thus my friend the poet Alexander Eremenko once wrote to me. Incidentally, here the caesura disappears after the third foot, as it does after the third shot.

6

There is yet another "testament" of the intelligentsia, also from Pushkin, about "secret liberty."

If "there is no joy," and "peace and freedom" are not to be had, then the only remaining options are collaboration with the prevailing ideology or "secret liberty," which, in literature toward the seventies, meant having nothing to do with anything.

Thus, in Russian poetry (and, on a broader plane, in Russian culture), two schools formed, two fundamental movements: *conceptualism* and *metarealism*.

7

The "sixties people" tried to bring back, let's say, "correct" social and cultural values, and in that sense they were our last romantics.

Conceptualism formed as a reaction to this "serious" approach and didn't try to prove anything to anyone. It merely "parodied" reality using reality's own language.

It was possible to relate to Soviet reality "tautologically"—that is, realistically—as if to a mechanism of oppression (which everyone at one time or another tested on himself). One could also try to explain, say, that Stalin, that's "bad," but Lenin, that's "good." Involuntarily, one ends up imitating the title of Maiakovsky's poem for children: "What is good and what is bad." And Rybakov, writer beloved of children, did just that "for adults." But around a certain time that approach seemed, at best, naïve.

But there was another way: to relate to Soviet reality as if to a mythology, to turn it inside out like a coat, to describe that very mythology with the help of its own semiotic system, and thus to show all of its indubitable absurdity. It turned out to be unbelievably funny. For example, Komar and Melamid's painting *Stalin and the Muses* shows Stalin, in his office, receiving the Greek Muses, who are appropriately attired. But it's only funny if you know what is being parodied; in this case, the very same picture in which Stalin receives some particularly productive milkmaids.

Or, say, a canvas entitled *Lennon and Children,* parodying the famous plot in Soviet mythology (especially prevalent in the graphic arts). A phonetic similarity in names became the means for exchanging one sign for another, provoked a Homeric chuckle, and promptly caused the painting to be yanked from an exhibition. Almost exactly the same thing was done in conceptual poetry. (Many conceptualists worked in both literature and painting.) Poetry merely replaced graphic clichés and stock icons with verbal ones, placed them in new contexts, and so forth.

Unfortunately, conceptualism depends completely on Soviet symbolism, which in the best of circumstances is only "half understood" by foreigners. Still, on the "western" side of the caesura, conceptualism enjoyed enormous success as straight-up sedition.

Now, when the caesura has disappeared and "Soviet" is only a mythology, parodying that "reality" no longer makes sense. Conceptualism must either die or degenerate into feuilletonism devoted to the loutish mug of Russian capitalism. But such things have already happened before in Russia, and so they have nothing to do with what's "new" in art.

8

"Conceptualism" was indeed a "new" word in Russian art and took its own place in that history. The conceptualists were, in essence, the opposite of the "sixties people," and in future literature textbooks they will, most likely, stand side by side.

Metarealism was a phenomenon of a different order, for it completely departed from *sotsum* as a theme.

Metarealism has been interpreted two ways: as "metaphysical realism" and as "metaphorical realism."

Metarealism can actually be called "the new Russian baroque," if only because at the foundation of its style lies "the metaphor," "the exaggerated detail." Of course, the baroque is not just "how"; it is also "about what." Metarealism tried to describe in baroque style a reality (or, more accurately, a number of realities) attainable only via the imagination and in no way connected with everyday existence (in Russian, *byt*). (I note parenthetically that the first instance of the plural form of "reality" was introduced by Gorbachev as, seemingly, a calque from English. This usage was less of a contradiction to the logic of Russian than to materialist philosophy, for which reality is singular. . . .)

Metarealism described society, but a society concerned with fish or dolls, and thus forced one to recall the *War Between the Mice and the Frogs* or Ariosto's "fantastic" passages. It is not as integral as conceptualism and in no way as bound by "theme" or "method" as the latter. Metarealism is more "literary" and more "international," and, therefore, I think, will not soon occupy a place in textbooks.

9

With perestroika, the Soviet underground immediately came out into the society of floodlights. Not having published a single line up to that point, authors rapidly received books and passage to places where they were known and had been translated even before perestroika. Many stayed there: some to teach, some to live. The critic who named conceptualism and metarealism now reads his own "short course" somewhere in the U.S.A. The caesura has disappeared. The Berlin Wall has fallen.

For Russian writers, a completely different life has begun.

10

At the beginning of this century, the great Russian poet Alexander Blok repeatedly returned to Pushkin's line: "All the world, all the world knows: / There is no joy." These guitaresque resettings seemed to my generation dreary and cheap "tautologies."

And the more profound "And eternal strife! Peace we only dream of / Through blood and dust" was yet another axiom of the "gypsy romance."

But deflowering (even of a caesura) does not occur without blood. And well and good if it's only metaphorical. . . .

Everything returns, and it's high time to cite Ecclesiastes.

11

Once this century, they took Russian history's temperature: 37 degrees Celsius, 38 degrees Celsius, 39 degrees, 40 degrees. When it hit 41, she all but died. . . . True, the Russian philosopher-eschatologist Berdiaev believed that history is in no way immortal.

I don't know what will become of Russian poetry. Poetry in general is a "luxury item," and, for the time being, there are problems with even the basics in the former Soviet Union. One consolation is that in Russia the biblical "In the beginning was the Word" is taken literally. To announce "capitalism" is much more important than actually to prepare for it. To this day, in Russia, it is considered enough just to say "From this day on we have capitalism" for it to start up, right then and there. . . .

It's exactly this faith in the word, however, and only this, that can explain the defeat of the August 1990 "putsch." After all, the putschists might have unceremoniously filled (using a "strong hand") Soviet stores. . . .

Tell me, what Westerner would go to his death on the barricades for an increase in prices?

But, again, everyone has it tough, and, again, the Russian writer is having a hard time living. If in the past publishing houses published "as per instructions" and "by agreement," now they aren't much for serious literature. . . .

And the Russian writer is becoming someone akin to the character (from Ilf and Petrov's novel *The Twelve Chairs*) Kisa Vorabianinov, who begged for alms in a southern spa with the words "*Monsieur, je ne mange pas six jours.* . . . Give something to a former deputy of the State Assembly." No, this isn't much of a time for literature in Russia. To somehow live through it—"Give to a

former writer"—that's the moan beginning to resound, little by lit-
tle, throughout the spas of capitalist Russia.

12

Here's yet another great Russian verse. About a blind man on a
church stoop. "And someone placed a stone in his outstretched
hand."

But while a new breed of collectors, recently brought to light,
trade a stone from the Berlin Wall for a finger broken off the mon-
ument to Dzerzhinsky (while it was being toppled from its pedes-
tal), we will remember that the Venus de Milo is eternally armless.

Simply put, the beautiful has nothing with which to beg
alms. . . .

13

What is Pushkin's verse-promise?

Correlating his "but there is peace, and freedom" with Blok's
"Peace we only dream of" would be enough material for another
set of notes. . . .

More and more, that line of Pushkin's seems to me something
like an hourglass: It depends on which side the thing is set down.

And an hourglass on its side—that's Faust's gesture: "Stay,
moment. . . ."

Translated by Peter Thomas

After the Future

Mikhail Epstein has been a pivotal figure in Russian (formerly Soviet) criticism since the beginning of the 1980s. He was among the very first to write on the Russian neo-avant-garde in poetry and, a bit later, in prose. This is how it happened.

In 1985 the major official magazine for literary criticism in the Soviet Union, *Voprosy literatury* (*Problems of Literature*), commissioned articles from two critics, Epstein and Igor Shaitanov, on recent trends in poetry known as conceptualism and metametaphorism, both of which had already been officially condemned (I was linked closely with the formation of the latter). When these articles were published, they turned out otherwise than the official literati had expected. According to Epstein and Shaitanov, we had seen the emergence of a new and unconstrained poetry as well as the birth of a new criticism. For the first time since the "Formalist" 1920s and the "scandalous" 1960s of Khrushchev's Thaw, Russian criticism was presented with complicated new material to analyze and from which to build up a new view of culture. American readers can get a sense of Epstein's ideas (although they will not be able to understand fully the cultural context in which they emerged) in his collection of essays entitled *After the Future*.

To understand this "alien" view better, one has to recognize some peculiarities of Russian approaches to critical writing. For example, Andrei Bitov, the famous writer and canonized martyr to Russian syntax, once described to me how, when translating a paragraph from John Locke to use as an epigraph for his novel, he had to employ twice as many sentences in Russian to make Locke's ideas clear. Was this because of the syntactical differences between the two languages? Not exactly. From the Russian perspective, English speakers, due, perhaps, to the "metonymical" nature of their language, are taught to explain their ideas in order to make them clear to almost everybody, while Russians, progeny of a "metaphorical" language, make their readers discern those ideas on their own in the course of their reading. Russians like to make their ideas sound like a *pun*, while Americans prefer to *pin* them up with logical development to some not less logical, even if paradoxical, conclusion. Vladimir Nabokov himself, who consumed pins as lances in his lifelong battle against butterflies, could not resist puns when writing in both Russian and English.

It would not be out of place here to ask whether national mentality is determined by language. My answer is affirmative. Hermann Hesse's *Glass Bead Game*, mentioned in passing in Epstein's book, is an example of what Russians believe any criticism is: a play on words and thoughts. While the Russian Formalists in the modernist period were still trying to explore the border between literature and "what is," Russian Formalists in the postmodern period, both in literature and in literary criticism (including Epstein), decided that "border" means "conflict." Conflict, while recognized from classical antiquity onward as the most powerful technique in art for its relation to catharsis, is not the only possible technique. For postmodernism, which seeks to make peace between contraries (to yoke together, as in the Russian fable, the lion and the doe), conflict as either device or border is obsolete, while the formal idea of a "game," even with "glass beads," is really what matters. The hero of Hesse's novel, by the way, never thought otherwise, and neither does Epstein—though he seems to object: "As distinct from Hesse's conservative and escapist Game, which is essentially derivative and forbids the creation of new signs and val-

ues, transculture aspires entirely to the sphere of creativity." I use
this unobliging quotation to illustrate the convergence of Epstein's
many neologisms in the term "transculture," by which he defines
and distinguishes his position. What is a "transculture" and who is
a "transculturist"? For Epstein,

> Transculture is the mode of existence of one liberated from
> nature by culture and culture itself by culturology. The trans-
> cultural world has never been extensively described because the
> path that leads to it—culturology, or the comparative study of
> cultures—was opened only recently. . . . The transcultural world
> lies not apart from, but within, all existing cultures, like a multi-
> dimensional space that appears gradually over the course of
> historical time. It is a continuous space in which unrealized,
> potential elements are no less meaningful than "real" ones. . . .
> Through the signs of existing cultures, a "transculturalist" tries to
> restore the mysterious script of the simultaneously present and
> absent transcultural condition. In essence, s/he both discovers
> and creates this realm. While scientists, artists, and politicians
> make significant but separate contributions to culture in their
> respective fields, the transculturist elaborates the space of trans-
> culture using various arts, philosophies, and sciences as tools to
> develop the all-encompassing genre of cultural creativity.

Epstein implies that the critic as "transculturalist" has the same
rights as any author to create an "unreal" equivalent to the "real" of
scientists, artists, and politicians—which, in turn, is the same "un-
real" in relation to everyday reality. In other words, "the critic is an
author" who is free to go in any direction "within all existing cul-
tures" that s/he wants. In the first place, Russian Formalists such as
Viktor Shklovsky and Iuri Tynianov already believed, in the mod-
ernist period, in the "equal rights" of critic and author, and were
writers as well as critics (compare French-American poststructur-
alism, where the critic is the only author who may be discussed).
Second, any direction "within all existing cultures" implies direc-
tions that are "existing," if perhaps not yet revealed (or, as Epstein
writes, "unrealized")—that is, the essence of any "conservative"
game, be it chess or glass beads. This direction will reveal, either
through literature or through criticism and philosophy, some
"new" reality about which we have only intimation. Here, Epstein
goes farther than the Formalists, who believed in the "new," in op-
position to the "old," values (language included) and thus was in

conflict with them. Unlike the Formalists, and like the Russian metametaphorists as well, Epstein knows that the "new" (including language) is a matter of combinations. It is what the game is about, and no other conflict than the tension of the game exists. The "transculturalist," who "us[es] various arts, philosophies, and sciences as tools to develop the all-encompassing genre of cultural creativity," seems thus emblematic of a postmodernist and post-Formalist paradox of pluralistic mastery.

Finally, we come back to where we started: the pun. Epstein's neologism also originates in pun; it is a "trans-culture" and a "culture of a trance," since both terms are spelled the same way in Russian. This is a culture that is able to foresee, through the contribution of language, its own "afterfuture," as if in a trance or in cyberspace. Thus, the Pan-Russian tradition (if you excuse the pun) is maintained: Epstein's terms do not just attract thought but are its very essence. *Pun* and *pin* are, in this sense, not just consonances but heads and tails of one and the same penny. The play on words at some point demands that the player set up some rules and start classifying in the new world. Adam gave names to what was created not by him and already classified by its creator; Linnaeus gave names to different plants and classified them, but they were not created by him, either. Borges, on the contrary, created and classified himself, but his classification touches only on his own creation and leaves no space for alien inventiveness. His type, of course, is close to that of Epstein's transculturalist, though far from Epstein's own ambitions.

Epstein's ambitions are very Russian, based as they are on the work of Dmitri Mendeleev, the inventor of the periodic table of the elements. It was Mendeleev who put all the known elements in good order, named those already discovered, and, even more important, predicted the existence of many as-yet-unrevealed elements by leaving space for them in his table. Epstein follows Mendeleev's path in creating what he calls the "Periodic Table of the New Russian Literature." On this table he places all Russian literature from 1730 to *F*, which he marks "1990–?" Of course, when he discusses the literature of earlier periods, Epstein uses terms already accepted (such as "classicism," "romanticism," and "acmeism"), but, for the new literature, he establishes some of his own. Thus he defines metametaphorism as composed of two branches, metarealism and presentalism (the present author, according to Epstein, belongs to the second category). Again, what is pinned down here are not just terms but also puns: "Metarealism," for example, encompasses both "metareality" and "metaphorical realism"; here, metaphor works as a compass to reveal metareality. Moreover, Epstein leaves blank spaces, as did Mendeleev, for directions in literature that are hard to imagine now, even if one is a transculturalist and a seer.

Epstein's position, in many respects, is an attempt to remain Mendeleev while becoming Borges; it is both a literary criticism that seeks science and a game that knows its own earnestness. After the future, both possibilities may occur.

Swedish Dialogue on Poetry

Poet Ilya Kutik and cultural scholar Mikhail Epstein had not seen each other for five years, long enough for a change not only of one's preferences but also of literary epochs. Their conversation is an attempt to become reacquainted with each other in a new time. Both had changed not just epochs but also their country of residence, having become faculty members in American universities. Their meeting in the city of Lund, in the south of Sweden, took place under the aegis of traditional Swedish neutrality and respect for the point of view of one's interlocutor. Indeed, the designation "Swedish" has become an established epithet in Russian in such contexts as a "Swedish table," a "Swedish family," a "Swedish wall," a "Swedish match," signifying high quality, ease, patience, and freedom from formal boundaries. Now we would like to introduce yet another, related meaning of the "Swedish discussion" or "Swedish dialogue," suggesting a rare tendency in the national tradition to get along without argument and, taking one's seat around a table, to round off any sharp corners in conversation.

Mikhail Epstein: Russian poetry, no longer an engine of social change and a refuge for all sorts of ideologies and mythologies, granted itself, as became apparent, the most difficult thing in poetry—that was to be no more and no less but exactly equal to its own needs and potentials. What is possible in contemporary poetry, and what is impossible—after Pushkin, Mandelstam, Brodsky, and even Prigov? Conceptualism revealed the sum of devices in Russian poetry, the array of its figurative clichés and traditions, and thereby made impossible their further use. What has happened—have the potentials of poetry narrowed or broadened? How can poetry live after the double death it experienced, having lost with glasnost its civic purpose and with conceptualism its figurative apparatus? How and why is it possible to do in poetry what you do in it?

Ilya Kutik: Your question really contains several. I think it's possible to answer some of them with the simple introduction of the more exacting epithet "Soviet," for Russian poetry, like any other, will never cease being a "refuge for ideologies and mythologies": In place of Soviet poetry other kinds will appear, and I'm not even so sure that the former will disappear. If one is to speak of social mythologies, then, to be sure, a Russian "mythology of capitalism" will appear. It will be that same Soviet mythology or, rather, its opposite. In that sense, conceptualism and postconceptualism are still possible wherever there is the right sort of time to play with. As concerns the exhaustion of devices and clichés, the achievement of conceptualism, the epithet "Soviet" is again appropriate. Conceptualism "revealed the sum of devices and clichés" of Soviet—well OK, Russian-Soviet—poetry, but part of Russian poetry of the Soviet period was not Soviet and remained Russian, that is, simply and before all else poetry, thriving by its deeper roots and tasks.

If we're speaking entirely retrospectively, then conceptualism not only debunks the device but is itself one of many devices that literature uses to displace entrenched totalitarianisms, even literary totalitarianisms. Such, for example, was the case in the nineteenth century, in the epoch of the totalitarian elegy. The "conceptualist" Iazykov appeared and used its clichés, laid bare its devices, and so forth, such that, it seems, the very genre itself should have been discredited for a long time. But then Benediktov arrived, began to write in the language of those very same clichés, mixed them with the diction of the eighteenth century, also totalitarian, but odic, and it turned out to be nothing if not novel and pluralistic, something which Russian poetry would have treated more attentively if it weren't for Vissarion Belinsky, the head of the single-partied nineteenth century.

The list of examples of this ebb and flow could be continued to this very day and forever. But the point isn't the examples. Rather, it's the laying out of the rhythm of literary breathing, the "preservation of distance," as Mandelstam put it. A distance runner won't start out as fast as a sprinter, since he has to run a long time. During that time, the spectators may disperse, drink beer, gossip, then return, but he'll still be running. The sprinter runs quickly and spectacularly, and conceptualism ran spectacularly to great "applause." And earlier, Evtushenko ran on that very same "civic" track on the long legs of "the sixties." But that track has been closed for repairs, and long legs are of no use if you have a sprinter's wind. It was the coach who focused on this type of race in the name of Soviet power. Soviet conceptualism was the same, only inside out, although "inside out" is always more productive; for with the help of the negation "not," all that is the same can be described, simply at greater length.

Therefore, to answer your question as to whether the potentials of poetry have broadened or narrowed, I can say just one thing—they've stayed just the same; that is, there are many. Poetry is not a pond that you toss a stone into, creating ripples of potentials, marks on a water gauge. And if you don't toss the stone, there aren't any. And if the pond is closed you can't go there at all. And the stadium of poetry isn't a pond, and it isn't a stadium. It's limbo à la Dante, where runners compete in their "green faith," which is green because it doesn't doubt its unwithering potential. Therefore, the figurative apparatus, as you put it, does not depend on Soviet or anti-Soviet mythologies, the essence of which is one and the same, but on much larger contexts.

It seems to me that poetry will soon outstrip all classifications that were once necessary to it. As Linnaeus did to earlier botany, so we will put to literary theoreticians questions of an entirely different order. One of these, for example, may turn out to be the necessity of a new science—of pleasure: about how from verse one receives satisfaction greater than that related to analysis and no less than that related to the culinary or sexual. What do you, as a theoretician, think about that?

M.E.: Enough has already been said about pleasure, beginning with Aristotle's theory of catharsis and ending with the famous tract of Roland Barthes, *The Pleasure of the Text*. Postmodernism, strictly speaking, brought to an end the pleasurable side of writing as a play of signs freed from their responsibility—or happiness?—to correspond to something besides themselves. Satisfaction without happiness? The right to semiotic satisfaction, granted by postmodernism, doesn't make us happier, because—it's the sad truth of postparadisiacal existence—happiness is somehow connected with labor, with the creation and transfiguration of reality, with the burden of responsibility, with the semantic load of the word.

I've always been struck that with the postmodernists there can be no lapses, poor lines, because there are no rules that they could break, no meanings to be expressed better or worse. In such poetry all is equally good—but is it good that all is equal?

I understand your refusal to speak to the most recent historical changes, but just the same I consider that with any new poet the potentials and even the nature of poetry changes. After Pushkin, it was already impossible to write like Derzhavin, or Karamzin, or Pushkin himself. Each new poet makes impossible in poetry precisely that which in him and through him became real and thus makes possible that which before him was impossible.

It seems to me that your verse system is one of the most self-reflexive in contemporary Russian poetry; that is, it accumulates many different cultural-historical layers and keeps them in their own associative fields. Therefore, the question of what is still possible in contemporary poetry after Brodsky and Prigov is directed precisely at you. Of course, you have some preferred points of reference in the past—Derzhavin, the ode, Baratynsky, Benediktov—but there is a geometric place for all points of Russian poetry from which a new poet tries to be equidistant in order to find a new place. And at that time, the center of gravity of the whole system changes; it slowly revolves in order to stop on another foundation. Each new poet knocks the system out of balance—and returns it to balance on a new place. Here is where the "pairing" of poetic names begins: Zhukovsky–Batiushkov, Pushkin–Lermontov, Tiutchev–Nekrasov, Maiakovsky–Esenin, Mandelstam–Pasternak, Akhmatova–Tsvetaeva. . . . Who is your other half, with whom do you maintain balance? It needn't necessarily be a single poet, but some system of counterbalances. . . .

I.K.: Yes, another pair: Evtushenko–Voznesensky . . . ; on the whole, it's an interesting question, pairing. But who is Brodsky's other half? Rein's? Or, since you've named him twice, Prigov's? But does the poet create a pair for himself, or, more likely, is it the wish of readers to construct a new Noah's Ark (where all are paired) so not to drown in a sea of poetry? But in it, you know, the sea, there are also solitary swimmers, and in general, the solitary swimmer (and his metonym, the sailboat) is a very popular topos in Russian poetry—it's in Zhukovsky, Pushkin, Iazykov, Lermontov, and many others, not just romantics. In the second half of this century, it seems that readers got into the habit of harnessing poets into troikas, creating a sort of Poseidon's trident, which is also connected to the sea. Evtushenko–Voznesensky, for example, is an incomplete combination, for in it—according to the will of the readers—Akhmadulina is missing. And whether she considers herself a part of that trident, it seems, is a question worrying no one, and no one asks her opinion. Who, then, is her pair? Sosnora? Aigi? Moritz?

But if you want pairs—by all means . . . for me that kind of pair is in many respects Alesha Parshchikov, and even the word "pair"—see for yourself!—exists in his very name. But I'm not at all sure that the future will agree with that pair and not, let's suppose, the pair Parshchikov–Zhdanov. Then you'll have to find me some other one.

But on the matter of counterbalance. True, I've always seen the historicism of poetry as a grand chessboard where the figures aren't as significant as the squares themselves, their black-and-white alternation. Sometimes the alternation "extends" for a century; sometimes it is briefer. Let's say that the eighteenth century was odic and the nineteenth elegiac. In the beginning of the twentieth century, there was a new turn toward the eighteenth century (Maiakovsky, Tsvetaeva, Pasternak, Zabolotsky, and others). In the second half of the century, there was a turn again toward the elegy (Brodsky, Akhmadulina, and I don't recall the many others on the order of Rubtsov). And again in the second half, which is already my generation, there was another (in a single century!) turn to the baroque tradition of the eighteenth century. This isn't the place to discuss all the twists and turns in that road, cluttered with signs to reduce one's speed, or the problem of the Russian classical baroque. It is much more interesting that poetry somehow balanced itself, using poets as ballast: Put one on the scale and remove another, and he's already gone, vanished. As it turns out—so as not to "vanish"—one needs to regulate one's weight category, so as always to make the needed weight, but that's already a question of poetic variety and, simultaneously, of the infamous "golden mean."

Right here is where your question arises on the psychological geometry within the writer, as he is writing, about how far he is from some points and how close he is to others. And now I won't get very far without ontology.

You recall, of course, that, according to Pascal, God is a sphere, the center of which is everywhere and the circumference of which is nowhere. And what is a sphere in philology if not the epic that, as Bakhtin wrote, may begin at any point, for it has always been beginning and won't ever end? For me, God is that epic, that is, the knowledge of much, even polar opposites, in one, as if a synthesis (if we speak of poetry) of everything were in it. And in that sense God is "postmodern," for in heaven there is no conflict, and the lion and the "trembling deer/doe" lie together there.

The poet is, according to an old and to this day just definition, a prophet: not one who "preaches," but one through whom, as through an antenna, transmission simply proceeds. Through one the epic is transmitted in the form of hexameters, through another—in the form of terza rima. For me (and this is not immodesty, but simply a lack of space, and you are asking me about me) the transmission proceeds by means of genre. Through it the Russian ode of the eighteenth century became for me the closest in Russian poetry to the epic, and to this day I feel it as a genre.

The epic is like parentheses, like two parted hands with an aura between them, but the hands brought together—it's a prayer, that is, a lyric poem. But poetry, you must admit, is still in its very essence more lyrical than epic, and I am most interested now in genres where the lyric and the epic seem to be harnessed together. This is, again, an experience of the "golden mean." But even in that sense, too, the ode as a genre is far from worn out, and the father of the term, Horace, as is well known, wrote odes in particular.

It seems to me that simply the generic quality in poetry (and poetry itself with it) will soon shift decisively. For example, (you're right!) how can one write elegies after Brodsky? He, of course, created an entire encyclopedia of "loss," the emotional-thematic foundation of the elegy. But that's just it, that genre still may deceive and, let's say, to name as an ode that which is manifest as an elegy, and vice versa, that's just what Brodsky did. And "to name" in poetry also means "to do."

That poetry which you christened "metarealism" is for me also a new potential of "Adamism," that is, of naming and describing those realities which exist but about which we know little, although we sense much. That is the expression of the "inexpressible," as you call it, or, paraphrasing the philosopher-Bolshevik, of that reality which we are given only in sensations but which is given to poets in images, rhymes, and genres.

But now do you sense that behind "metarealism," as its godfather, there are some new potentials, or have you given your godchild the last rites? Do you feel that his role has already been played out? Unsuccessfully? Successfully? Succeeding?

M.E.: Along with metarealism (metaphysical realism) I had still another term that had signified the "golden mean." That middle style was denominated by me as "presentalism," a poetry of the genuine. This is at once the thinnest and thickest level of phenomena, lying between transcendental worlds, toward which the metarealists strive and from which the Conceptualists estrange themselves. Presentalism affirms the "beingness" of its topoi without drowning them in otherworldliness or unworldliness. This is a poetry not of the countenance and not of the mask but of what is in front of our faces in the universe.

But that doesn't mean that it keeps to plainly objective spheres, toeing the line of a realistic order and not allowing itself a step either right or left. It is sooner a boat that rocks to both sides, only not allowing itself to capsize, take on water, sink into the depths or to fly off into the heavens. Presentalism is a poetry of balance, guarded from within, so that any emotional lapse is immediately righted by a gesture to the opposite side.

For example, your "Ode" is presentalist not in the sense of strictly observed objectivity (which would be an accurate appraisal of the fulfillment of a seventy-year maximal program of

acmeism), but in that the odic soaring itself contains deflating sty-
listic gestures.

> That first one [wind] chased a tidal wave through Marathon,
> but here in heavy daubs the seas
> in sleep can merely put their makeup on.

The odic "Marathon" is balanced by the jargonistic "makeup,"
but raised into the singular deity Tsunami (tidal wave) it rhymes
with *zhirnymi mazkami* (heavy daubs) from the arsenal of the
courtesan shimmering like the sea. The rule of such poetry is to
roll with all its strength but in no instance to overturn.

If we are to speak of a new aesthetic category that it embodies,
and it would be worthwhile now at the end of the twentieth cen-
tury to introduce and understand it, then it would be *resilience*. Of
all physical characteristics, it is the least of all understood. "Resil-
iency" signifies the measure of recoil inside a pressure such that a
resilient object, in contrast to the hard or soft (listless), itself pro-
vides a push opposite to that given. Presentalism is the aesthetic of
resiliency: Each image contains associative chains pulling it in op-
posing directions. Each image is the recoil opposite to the shot.

I.K.: As for the spring—that's still "true," anyway, in another
sense, and we discussed it time and again in our poetic group. Be-
neath the spring, the same lyric poem was implied, for it shoots,
like a spring, only a single time. It "lives" at the expense of a greater
context not created by it, beginning in antiquity. Thus, to give an
example, ancient Greek lyrics lived "at the expense" of the Hom-
eric epic, and so forth. This led to the desire to create one's own
"great" plan, in order later to chop it into pieces of lyrics. But why
a spring, returning to the chains of images of our beginning, and
not the rings of Dante and not a stadium?

But lyric and epic are genres. Do you consider that something
still flows in them, or, in your opinion, is the generic potential ex-
hausted and there is nowhere to go with it?

M.E.: It is precisely the entropic character of being totally
mixed, inherent in the postmodern, that now demands the acuity
and sobriety of generic consciousness. You see, there are such
genres within which the confusion of genres itself takes place ac-
cording to generic rules and gives birth to the energy of a multi-
composite image, such as, for example, the lyric-epic genre of the

ballad. I've already mentioned to you that after our last telephone conversation, before today's meeting in Lund, I experienced some sort of pre- or postsleep state that in English is called a lucid dream, in which I clearly heard that the Ilya who so gloriously began with "The Ode" should in the interim turn to the ballad. That's already your good fortune—to elevate generic designations to their own names.

For the ballad, it appears to me, is that "narrow" path by which the contemporary poet may get out of the dead end described above of "poetry without rules and without sails." If, in your words, the elegy ended for us with Brodsky, then the ballad in its own new postromantic character still has not begun, if we don't consider several poems of Olga Sedakova and Ivan Zhdanov that are named ballads. But those are ballads only nominally, inasmuch as they are missing the main property of the ballad—a plot. They are lyrical sprouts of balladic thought called to become something big, to stand at the crossroads of plot and metaphor.

The ballad is a poetically conscious gesture in the direction of postmodernism, a gesture of agreement with it and an overcoming of it by the rules of the genre. The ballad makes poetry sound of mind, returns to it the feeling of plot, temporal continuity, narrativity—but without those cumbersome and difficult-to-read forms that plot acquired in the thoroughly developed narrative poem (and all the more so in the novel in verse). The contemporary ballad is Goethe read through the eyes of Hitchcock and translated into the language of Borges. The ballad is ambiguous, dark, mysterious, squeezed into the frame of a clear plot, the margins illustrated with ancient monograms of Middle Ages half authorship and postmodern flight from authorship.

And for you personally, it is moreover the possibility of mooring to the shore and, with the maritime space of your "Ode," of entering the wooded thicket of the ballad. The ballad is related to the ode as the woods are to the sea. In the ode there is the space of the exalted, in the ballad the drowsy interweaving of the mysterious. The song becomes a whisper. But there already opens a desert of silence, too, where you would like to cast a glance with your final book. . . .

Let it all turn out differently, but I would like that possibility, perhaps purely theoretical, to be inculcated into your poetry, precisely at its present point of growth, as its own possibility, as a theoretical work having arisen on its foundation.

I.K.: I don't know. For me the ballad provides a definitive harmony between poetry and prose, but in the end, perhaps, I understand too little to "balance" it. . . .

Since you've already mentioned Borges, however, some sort of new form of poetic essayism is probably possible. It might be called the contemporary ballad. And it seems to me that in that genre we could, in principle, equally excel.

Translated by Justin Weir

On Reading Aigi

Emptiness—God's body. . . .
—Ilya Kutik

1

I propose behaving calmly toward this thought: Verse is unnecessary to anyone. . . . I have *our* art in mind. . . . It was unnecessary in the fatherland of Russian verse—earlier (*because* . . .), and it is unnecessary now (also *because* . . .). It is also unnecessary in other fatherlands of poetry. I repeat. I am speaking of verse-*art*. . . . It is (and will be) necessary to have verse-Marseillaises, verse-appeals (to somewhere), verse-feuilletons, and such, but not *verse*. . . .

And there is nothing terrible about that.

It is worth making a proviso, however: Verse is necessary to he (they . . .) who writes it himself (even when it is "without a pen"). The poet reads other verse *as* a poet; that is, not as a reader; that is, egoistically; that is, seeking something *there*, for him.

2

What is most "strange" is that Aigi is nearly impossible to read, egoistically, but as a *reader* I, too, am unable. . . . So then what? . . .

3

And I will answer.

Aigi's verse must be read while stripped naked, the windows open, allowing for drafts. And then you will experience the *lightest* shiver, first on one part of skin, then on another, first here, then there. . . .

The prickle of goose bumps . . .

And another thing. Leaning out a window, to smoke, let's say, you may feel the curtain (tulle), blown slightly by the wind, strike your shoulder. . . . It is penetrating, like a caress during the total absence of a caresser, the consolation of the inconsolable. Penetrating, and the heart aches. . . .

4

The heart aches—*always*. For a long, long time I considered inordinately romantic the aphorism of the German about how *the fissure of the world passes through the heart of the poet*. Now I sense it, even naturalistically. . . .

Let's take, for example, an apple. Cut it (it may open up itself, if it has *ripened*). The cut oozes and then begins to darken, more and more. And thus the *space* between Aigi's words *darkens*. And you'll do nothing. The fissure of the world passes through the heart of the poet. But whence the *words?* . . .

5

The words . . . sometimes it is said that Aigi's texts are reminiscent of crosswords. That is so. The word for horror, for example, or for pain . . . and don't bother looking at the back of the book. There are remarks and commentaries there, but there is no *answer*. . . . Be intelligent and steadfast, you'll give your own. . . .

6

At first, it seems that Aigi's verse lives beneath the epigraph (the "roof") of another great poet. *I've forgotten the word.* . . . And the "recollections" begin, a duel in the air. "In azure the splinter agonized. . . ."

In the novel *The Pharaoh*, by Prus, there is a brilliant "metaphorical situation." Many different people—dying, suffering, fighting wars, creating—pray simultaneously. Their prayers are carried up to the Creator, but they collide in the air, scatter, and do not reach Him. And only a single prayer—that of a child—shoots up directly to God, because it was not for the child but *for all*, and therefore it did not collide with the others. The Creator hears it, and (for a moment) peace descends on the world, and, at that moment, *all* suffering ceases. . . .

Reading Aigi's verse, I get the sensation that *one* of the words is always *required*—it reaches God, and therefore Aigi is a great poet. His verse is like *that* prayer: not *for* himself but *from* himself.

7

But is that *sensation* proof? Yes, it is! It depends on one's *ear*, however, on whether the reader has an organ perceiving poetry. . . .

It is strange, but Aigi's is nearly the only verse I can reread endlessly, each reading sending chills through different parts of my skin than before.

One of my poet friends somehow noticed perspicaciously that a poem is a "spring of a single act." It actually "shoots" just once. The rest is already a matter of whether you are a "gourmand"; that is, the "shot" can be savored as often as you like.

With Aigi, it is not quite the same. You savor from him not the shot but something else; to remain alone with his verse is to smoke in solitude, anxious, endless, with that very same *caress* of the curtain. . . .

8

It is possible (of course, possible) to say of Aigi much that is scholarly and wise. . . . But sometimes reading much of this sort about him, you feel like a golfer waiting for hours to tee up, or a "glass bead player." Poetry, of course, is also a "glass bead game" (but what isn't?), but in it there is *prayer*.

9

Just the same, there is the question of "productiveness." What may a poet take for himself *from* Aigi, except *sensations?*

Perhaps the *sole* thing is the ability to orient oneself *there. . . .*

Once my pal and I wanted to "try" this situation: Gather together several people born in the same city and ask each to draw the map that he (or she) sees while dreaming. For cities, especially one's native city, are often dreamed of. On the dream map (*certainly*), there will be some of those streets which exist in the "real" city, but (*certainly*) there will also be those streets, squares, and little alleys whose essence is *only* in a dream. . . . The most interesting thing is whether the "maps" correspond. If yes, then there is your Augustine, that same *"there."*

My pal and I failed to create such a "situation." Aigi does create that map. . . . And he knows this himself ("I know *that* there"). In my view, Malevich (Aigi's favorite) was also just such a cartographer.

Aigi and the "dream"—that's his, Aigi's, theme (probably also the theme of future "dissertations"). But that *map* is much more complex (and "simple") than one simply "seen in a dream," and Aigi's verse is in no way a key for the map, or a guide or compass (like this essay—in no way a review of books coming out or already published by Aigi). . . .

I'll say it this way: Aigi creates a *labyrinth*, but Daedalus cannot be, simultaneously, Ariadne, too. Aigi's verse is not *its* thread—to repeat, it is a *labyrinth*.

A labyrinth is a means of *organizing* space, that which we roughly and clumsily call by various names ("air," "emptiness," "nothingness," . . .), like the ancient Jews, for whom it was *impossible* to name *one thing*. . . . (Not in vain did Daedalus, having built and organized it, escape *there*.) Precisely *that sort* of organization, in my instance, also means: *that* I may "draw from" Aigi.

10

For the first time, after having "collided" with Aigi's verse, I understood that it is possible if not to *name* then to *describe* "impossibility" (if you like, "absence"), that is, as though to reconcile the *horror of emptiness* (from, say, "Gethsemane Garden" of Nerval) with the most *steadfast faith*.

Here, for example: "When the world like 2 × 2 = 4 / and the all-encompassing without (and to finish with that very Without)." One sees the same thing in the pictures of Igor Ganikovsky.

Ganikovsky has one called *The Triumphal Arch*. In the picture, there is the usual "triumphal arch," such as there is in Moscow, and in Paris, and wherever you like, and even near Gogol's Dikanka (what broom swept it there?). But *alongside* the very arch on the canvas there is nothing, it "stands" in *empty* canvas, and that which *should* be alongside and nearby—Ganikovsky has "swept" *inside* it.

The arch *is supported* by emptiness.

It cannot be "deflowered," not by a Roman triumph or by somebody's parade. . . . It is as though it lives by its own *visions*, like the eternal virgin Joan of Arc—by its own *voices*. . . .

"And the cloak of the Paris or Brandenburg gates / was thrown off the shoulders of time," I wrote then.

Something very *concrete*—from *nowhere*. Like love, for example.

11

How strange it is that Aigi and Mandelstam so often echo one another. Mandelstam wrote that what is important to him is not the bagel but the hole in the bagel. You can eat the bagel, but the hole remains. . . . Or: "Real labor is Brussels lace. The main thing is that upon which the design relies: the air, the pinholes, and the absences. . . ."

There are, in essence, only *two* means of description (of a man, feeling, or whatever you like). The first is the *direct* portrait; the second is the "portrait" of that which *surrounds* the direct portrait. Like an icon pulled from its frame. Aigi's verse (his *method*) belongs to the second category.

The description of the feeling "I love," say, as that which is *by* "I love" is only a strengthening of the very "I." And that is not "minus" individuality but almost *epic*, only within the "confines" of the lyric. And that is the great lyrical discovery of Aigi.

Therefore, to speak of Aigi's verse is to encircle (*kruzhit'*) it (from the word "lace" [*kruzhevo*]), that is, to speak of that which *surrounds* it.

Therefore, it is also impossible to "illustrate" Aigi's verse directly but only and just only as it was brilliantly done, for example, by Nikolai Dronnikov in two Paris books: with the apportionment of the letter, line, and *distribution* of the text. That is, through the organization of *space*. Or as Igor Vulokh does it: with lines distributed differently within set limits of the page, but as though *splitting* it. . . .

12

Aigi loves to describe that which is impossible to name, what is impossible also to describe. Thus Rimbaud, in his own words, "stumbled" on the description of "indescribable states," such as "dizziness" and so forth. But he *pushed* them in a quotidian direction, trying to "understand" them from *ecstaticness*. Aigi provides for them in verse, as though (*suddenly*) groping for that *point* where the "tunnel" of those states begins.

I am convinced that the "conversation" of the world is formed from some sort of dotted lines of radiation released even by silent objects; at some *point* those rays intersect, and it is necessary only to understand, sense, *intuit*, that point in order to "enter" onto that universal conversation. . . . And it is not at all necessary to study an iota or to eat a "broth of wonders," like some kind of sorcerer.

For me, that *point* is called *genius*.

13

Aigi is perhaps the most "metaphysical" of today's Russian poets. What is more, the "meat," thingness, baroque elements (if you like) in his verse are absent, but the "theme" is always an elevated one. They (the "meat" and so forth) appear as a system that necessarily "lowers" the elevated (for without "lowerings" the elevated couldn't be sensed; it would be like a "plus" on a "plus"), which Aigi "lowers" in an altogether *different* fashion, speaking "literally": with drops (and jumps) in syntax, with spaces, with oblique language—both simpleminded and specialized.

14

I don't want to discuss the great "teachers" of Aigi. Much has been said about them by Aigi himself and by others. But there is a single name I would still like to mention. That is Cyprian Norwid. "He's the one for whom," Mandelstam would have said, "absences breathe. . . . Brussels lace lives! . . ."

15

"When the world like $2 \times 2 = 4$ / and the all-encompassing without (and to finish with that very Without)."

That's from "Reading Norwid" by Aigi. . . .

Reading Aigi . . . "(*and to finish with that very Without*)." Or, perhaps, from the same place: "When—longing—living—leaves—provinces."

O, no! I will answer for him. For *longing* (*toska*) to escape (to heaven) is eternal (as *eternally* the heart aches; ". . . say, *My naked heart* again"—as Aigi says—for himself, for Baudelaire and Norwid, *for* all of us). . . .

Which is just to say, if you *have* the lace, you have his *breath.* . . .

In principle, this is also, to us, an *answer*—"through waftings—as if from the entire emptied, severe Earth. . . ."

16

Like: . . . a curtain . . . tulle . . . a touch on the shoulder . . .

Lund, June 1992, night
Translated by Justin Weir

Invitation to the Sentimental

1

Until recently, the relationship of the Russian poet to his readers has been that of "a prophet among mortals." "A writer among those who read him"—this is the relationship today. Concert halls and kitchens, those Indian reservations of the Russian intelligentsia, those self-styled Hyde Parks for the rhymes and rhythms of clairvoyants, have finally been given back to their primordial vocations, to concerts and dirty (clean) dishes. Poetry, too, has finally taken its own place, which is to say, it is being written and published, if only on lousy paper. So is it really worthwhile talking about poetry's future, more likely boring (like its flaccid worldwide present) than titillatingly adventurous? Not at all like the career of the Count of Monte Cristo, who grew hairy and unkempt in prison, ran along "the shores of desert breakers," found a bushel of money, and set off, a smoothly shaven and pleasant smelling fop, to avenge himself on his offenders. Is this "boring" future really worth discussion at all?*

---

*The given observations do not extend to those extraliterary phenomena of artificially overcome boredom so well suited to the yawning epoch

It is, because boredom is an aesthetic oven, and even though it's cold, we nevertheless have to warm up there. And that stove, our starting point, sits in some sort of unintelligible gap, a gap unprovided for in the floor plan and, therefore, apparently nonexistent, despite the unquestionable existence of the stove. Here I'll cite Pasternak's translation of Verlaine (which, however, has little in common with Verlaine) concerning "ennui," that somewhat cantankerous little sister of upstanding boredom:

> Ennui out of no place,
> But ennui just the same,
> Bad times aren't the problem
> And good's not to blame.

There it is, the gap, that inexplicable "between," worthy of good metaphysical binoculars. And Russian poetry has found itself in that gap for the impending future, fearing boredom like some kind of Buddhism.

Russian history slammed its index finger in the door some time between the 1380 victory at Kulikovo and the victory of 1480 and was numb for a full hundred years. For some reason, to this day it still points toward Ivan the Terrible (in Russian, Ivan Groznyi) or to the Chechen capital. If not history, then at least literature ought to come out of "gaps" without black-and-blue fingers.

2

Let's start with a "gap" more intelligible to literature and with our latest—chronologically speaking—poetic classic.

Brodsky, as is well known, preached "healthy classicism" and contrasted it with "sarcasm." (See the poem "To a Poetess.") Breaking down what he actually meant by the former and the latter is not the ambition of this essay. I'm interested in what sits "between" them. We'll go with the flow.

---

of Brezhnevian timelessness and clinging inertially to the stage even today, in the epoch of chaotic capitalism and aesthetic boredom. These "currents," having no readers due to their inherent unreadability and losing their last listeners like a crowd-working lounge lizard on the eve of retirement, reaffirm the ancient OPOYAZ thesis that a repeatedly repeated device undoes its own author.

"Healthy" classicism of the eighteenth century was fast friends with sarcasm, as is also well known. For proof of that, it's enough just to know, without even having read it, that Alexander Pope wrote *The Dunciad* (1728–42). So why does Brodsky argue that they are in opposition? The whole matter has to do with "health." Sarcasm grows unhealthy when it pours itself into masks and gesticulations or into affectation. "Healthy" sarcasm is simply the healthy organism's reaction to "this isn't pleasing," in recognition of other, larger tasks. The mask comes from a different wardrobe belonging to romanticism. It's the last thing the poet takes off before bed and the first thing he reaches for before breakfast. Only the pillow knows his real face, and then only if he sleeps alone. Classicism amused itself at real, costly carnivals, and steered clear of glued-on masks.

But there is a more subtle continuation here as well. The transition from romanticism to realism—by way of the mask—is much more direct than is usually thought. The noted "psychologism" of the Russian nineteenth century in fact never removed its mask. Instead, as is fitting for this successor and equal (in might) to Greek tragedy, it provided itself with two masks. When a sorrowful situation would arise in a work, the psychological hero would act "contrarily," donning the mask with the corners of the mouth pointed up; if the situation demanded laughter, the corners twisted down. Of course, I'm simplifying things. The hero of literature in the period of "psychologism" is already not the author's absolute double. But the essence of "psychologism" is also masked. Classicism, insofar as it was healthy, refrained from excess of tears and excess of laughter, not without reason befriending Horace's "golden mean": Nothing in excess, all in moderation.

So let's sum up. Classicism—romanticism (with psychologism continuing its content in realism and avant-gardism extending its form). What is in between, in the place marked by that linking dash? In the place between "nothing in excess" and "too much"? There's no point in thinking too much about it: "naturalness," the immediate, that is, the most healthy reaction.

And this "health" is the link's primary weakness. For although people are much more complex than literature, every person who cries literarily when times are sad, and anyone who laughs literarily when times are happy, seems to "developed" literature much

more unnatural than the most unnatural reaction (that is, the op-
posite of what is called for). Naturalness in literature is naïve, like
a child among adults, and the handbook of lit-trends has labeled it
"sentimentalism." That's what is at issue. . . .

3

. . . For poetry, it seems, is coming into an epoch of "new" sentimen-
talism, what Mandelstam might have called "that mean skillfully
found between the classical and the romantic manner" ("Remarks
on Chenier"). It is interesting to ask why.

What is the difference between Goethe's great "Mignon," with her

> Dahin! Dahin
> Möcht ich mit dir, o mein Geliebter, ziehn

(so wonderfully rhyming with the Russian *vy-dokhni* [exhale] and
ot-dokhni [rest]), and this call from Baudelaire's "Invitation au voy-
age"?

> Mon enfant, ma sœur,
> Songe à la douceur
> D'aller là-bas vivre ensemble!

The difference between Goethe's "dahin" and Baudelaire's is
that the first calls to the "there" of the exotic ("Kunst du das Land,
wo die Zitronen blühn, / Im dunkeln Laub die Goldorangen glühn, /
Ein samfter Wind vom blauen Himmel weht, / Die Myrte still und
hoch der Lorbeer steht . . ."), whereas the second calls to the "there"
of comfort ("Des meubles luisants, / Polis par les ans, / Décoreraient
notre chambre . . ."). Goethe's landscape "there" is also comfort-
able in its own way, but it is all about the azure-unattainable and
the romantic, while Baudelaire's comfort "there" is quite "here,"
healthy and even almost bourgeois, with its furniture, flowers in
vases, and mirrors on the walls. One "dahin" is about breaking out
of here, "exhaling"; the other is about, well, "dahier," "resting,"
about breaking into the "hierher" from the romantic and already at-
tained generic-poetic "thither." A strange poem for Baudelaire, but
entirely in correspondence with today's mood in poetry.

4

For poetry is sick of striving and wants to become "vulgar." Not in the sense that it will be intended for vulgarians (as it was in the time of Nadson and Sully Prudhomme, in the epoch of sots-sentimentalism, and as it remains in places where the pink ribbon of soap opera peaks through). Rather, in the sense that it would finally like to see the ground it is standing on, clear off a bit for itself, and set up a home there, with a cat (still a trademark of both Baudelaire and comfort). And also a snow-white computer with the Internet, the cerebral adventurer's substitute for Lermontov's sail.

And we need sail nowhere further ourselves when all "flags" are sailing to us of their own volition, when the world has narrowed to fit a tiny screen and spread out to contact any who can afford it. For the first time, the mountain and Mohammed finally meet, rather than waiting to see who'll take the first step.

The consequences for poetry in cyberspace are also immediate. Or, more precisely, for what we are accustomed to call the poetic imagination.

With cyberspace the world paradoxically "becomes divine" because the Net assures us a dialogue with people who virtually aren't. That is, they exist, but in such a degree of abstraction and at such distance that, taken as a whole, they seem to be a metaphor and at the same time evidence of otherworldly being. With cyberspace it's all so obviously literal that no better illustration for Dantesque adventures comes to mind to abolish the infernal Doré.

5

Again, I'll quote Mandelstam, still the best Russian essayist of the twentieth century (from "On the Collocutor"):

> The unexpected is the air of verse. Faced with the known, we are able to say only what is known. . . . The poet is only bound to the providential collocutor. . . . True, when I am talking to someone, I don't know that person and can't hope to know him. There is no lyric without dialogue. . . . There is no sense in worrying

about acoustics: They will come on their own. Worry about distance. It's boring to whisper with one's neighbor.

And from "Fourth Prose": Poetry is "stolen air."

Even if this isn't "stolen air" in Mandelstam's sense—illicit, snatched from breathing's stuffiness—nonetheless, the functional community between poetry and the Internet is obvious. And the issue isn't whether verse will soar in the weightlessness of cyberspace. It already does, as it always has, even before Dante, that interviewer from the nonexistent medieval BBC, climbing right into Hell. Even before Swedenborg searched for information in precomputer cyberspace and was considered, because of these "searches," at worst a madman and at best merely a poet. The metaphysics of cyberspace is not abolishing and will not abolish the poetry of books. But then poetry—by the medium's very existence—no longer needs to try to prove that God is, just as for some time now there has been no need to send rockets into space to prove that God is not.

6

Finally, poetry can return to its domestic responsibilities, and return us to the lowly (or exalted—to each his own) gastronomic, intestinal happiness that poetry is obliged to provide. Poetry is foremost a pleasure which cannot be formulated but which touches and moves our *sens*. That is why the pleasure of poetry is sentimental. The golden apple of paradise, which knows no shadow, and the black wings of Satan, who has just alighted—one ought to speak not about the genius of color contrast in Milton's image but about the pleasure to which that contrast drives us. "To tears," in this case, is not testimony to some unusual upset of the tear ducts (as "onion" tears, for example, do not implicate cookery in some new form of torture). On the contrary, it speaks of the reader's more elevated preparedness to make use of the limits established in art. Poetry must discover Aristotle anew, as Columbus discovered America after the Scandinavians. Poetry must understand that "catharsis"—which is the furnishing of happiness and not "what" or "how"—is its main goal and only justification. Not to derange the senses, à la Rimbaud, but to move them.

So that turning each page is like cutting through an onion. So that every time we read through a poem, our eyes warm, like our fingers when we touch a lover's skin.

7

And again, about boredom. Boredom, which is the condition of a spiritual "gap," can be quite productive if "correctly" addressed, that is, not as inactivity but rather as a different form of concentration. A different, more equal distribution of spiritual strengths and accents. As in cyberspace. As in my beloved Tomas Tranströmer's "milking the cosmos, little by little." "The night sky lows and does not calve. We milk the cosmos, little by little, and survive."

Russian poetry is bored because it has been deprived of its social activism and has not yet found domestic comfort. It finds the state of Western poetry boring because the Russian has a hard time (and, for the time being, no possibility of) imagining that measure of life by which one changes pipes and tobaccos according to the day of the week, rather than having to polish off the wine cellar in a single day.

It's also difficult to work out an aesthetic relationship to boredom because of the absence of worthy models. (We'll leave aside the ingenious Chekhonte; and we can't use Chekhov himself, that Russian dramatist for foreigners and founder of soap opera as world genre!)

Russian poetry is ingenious and keenly understands matters when the issue is extremes: Either "ecstasy in battle and at the dismal chasm's edge" (Pushkin), or the sweet comforts of "life at Zvanka" (Derzhavin). Quotidian colorlessness it finds impotent and unproductive, only good for a cycle of elegiac complaints. But, meanwhile, such a model in art does exist.

The films of Wim Wenders—here is a template of strained languor, lassitude driven to genuine Greek catharsis, the contemporary artist's reference manual for turning boredom into gold. I'll mention only one film, *The Order of Things* (1982), in which boredom is the primary unit of measure and catharsis is achieved in the most unexpected way.

A certain director is filming. The film ends, and everyone waits for the producer. He's nowhere to be found. Everyone waits for him. They languish. They take strolls, play the violin, run their eyes over objects. Boredom is intense: The producer still isn't there. And that's ninety percent of the film. Finally (and Wenders places this right at the finale), the director goes to look for the producer. He searches. (The tempo picks up.) He finds him. (The tempo speeds up sharply.) It turns out that the producer is hiding from someone. They are both being murdered (by whom and for what is not important). That's it. The end of the film. When the teakettle comes to a boil, they turn it off. They turn on the lights in the cinema.

Catharsis proved possible because boredom made the not-plot stronger. The not-plot wanted to break out of boredom aesthetically. Likewise, the plotlessness of what we are used to calling humdrum existence is always delivered by some event, be it our own death or the purchase of an automobile. Or a poem.

8

What I'm talking about has simple, worldly equivalents. If things are going badly for someone, he either hits the bottle (the Russian variant) or loses himself in work (the Western variant). If some unexpected encouragement spurs him on, he either hits the bottle again (Russian variant) or works even harder (Western variant). If everything is "just OK," he (Russian variant) just drinks or (Western variant) just works. Russian poetry, finding itself "in a bad way" until the mideighties, and "unexpectedly encouraged" during the brief gap between then and the early nineties, in both cases stayed hammered. The "just OK" situation is tough—it's still *Russian* poetry—but we'll have to turn to the Western variant.

9

... And Vera Pavlovna has a dream. People wear golden pants, like angels. Tigers in prisoners' uniforms pad unfettered. No one understands metaphor, but mountain goats, peering into the water, see their horns bifurcated, like mermaids' tails. Lyres gather dust in the corner, like distaffs today and computers—tomorrow. Beds of onions are overgrown with roses. Wars require no Homer, peace no Hesiod.

In the ideal state, where poets, according to Plato, have no place, the last poets' last possibility is to become "onions."

Translated by Peter Thomas

PART II

On Swedenborg and Other Matters

In Asia Minor or in Alexandria, in the second century of our faith, when Basilides disseminated the idea that the cosmos was the reckless or evil improvisation of deficient angels, Nils Runeberg would have directed, with singular intellectual passion, one of the Gnostic conventicles. . . . Instead, God afforded Runeberg the twentieth century and the university town of Lund.

—Jorge Luis Borges, "Three Versions of Judas"

Verlaine's Violin

For some time now I've wanted to write this story, but could never figure out how to go about it. The story lacked a backdrop, or what we sometimes call a melody. By the way, anyone who has visited or lived in Scandinavia knows that the main melody here is one played on the violin, and it matters not at all the season: It is always weepy and overcast, like a violin concert in a dark hall. At the time (that is, when I had just arrived in the northern part of Europe), the same lines by Verlaine went through my head over and over. The poem was perfectly suited to the state of my soul and the weather. Actually, it wasn't the whole poem (I don't know it all), but just the very beginning of it:

> Les sanglot longs
> Des violons
> De l'automne
> Blessent mon coeur
> D'une langueur
> Monotone.

At the beginning of this poem, entitled "An Autumn Song," there is a surprising and contradictory line which can be understood in at

least two ways. There are numerous Russian translations of this
line, this strophe, and of this whole poem, but they possess only
limited ways to deal with the mysterious duality of the Verlainian
image. Therefore, I will cite only two examples. The first belongs to
Valery Briusov:

> The long plaints
> Of autumnal violins,
> Their tormenting call
> Wounds my heart,
> Clouds my thoughts,
> Unceasingly.

The second is a contemporary translation by Alexander Revich:

> Autumn, tormented
> By dreary violins,
> Is wracked by sobs,
> So monotonous
> Are its wails and moans,
> That my heart hurts. . . .

Since we are not discussing the quality of the translations but
rather the magical duality of Verlaine's verse, we can note that in
both translated verses this duality is obvious. In the first case, the
image exists as an "autumnal violin," while in the other, one gets it
as "autumn's violin." The difference is huge, but nonetheless it is
difficult to grasp: One might explain it semantically, but to feel it
(which is what, really, a poetic image ought to make us do) is al-
most impossible.

And so begins my story, which happened about five years ago
during one of nature's frequent violin concerts. A man with a violin
walked onto the platform of the train station in Copenhagen. Inas-
much as this is a true story, I won't get caught up in the details of
the portrait, such as his size or clothing. It suffices to say one thing:
This man was a clown who had come to Copenhagen from Baku,
and his baggage consisted of a suitcase and a violin. How this fel-
low made it from the train station to the hotel, how he unpacked
his suitcase, and so forth—all that is more in the realm of belles
lettres, which is to say, so much guesswork, and therefore I won't
delve into the details. What is known for certain is that that very
evening, the clown (and that's how we'll refer to him—the clown)
phoned two music experts in Copenhagen and asked to meet them.

Everything that happened afterward is known to me through one of these experts, and I will stick closely to his version of the events.

When both of these experts arrived in the hotel room where the clown was staying, the latter, in their presence, opened up his case and took out his violin. He requested both of them to examine the instrument closely. The reaction of both experts was the same: They froze in disbelief and holy trembling, for the violin which they held in their hands was a Stradivarius. After five years, it's a bit difficult to recall all the details that one of the participants in this amazement disjointedly related to me. I can't remember exactly how many Stradivariuses are known to be in existence: something like eight or nine or twelve. In any case, the clown's violin made one more violin by the great Italian, and, what is more, it wasn't included in the quite small tally of these priceless instruments. So the clown (and this isn't surprising) asked the experts how much the violin was worth, in other words, whether one might sell it in Copenhagen. When both the experts decisively declared this impossible, since Stradivariuses are priceless, the clown put the violin back in the case and thanked them for the advice. Before he left, the expert who told me this story timidly asked the clown how he had come into possession of the extra Stradivarius. The clown meekly answered that he had found it in an attic in Baku and that, although he realized that it was old, he had had no idea of the instrument's uniqueness.

According to one of the witnesses of the violin, he couldn't sleep that night but rather relived the meeting in all of its details, alternately believing and disbelieving whether the meeting had really taken place. Early the next morning, he called the clown at the hotel and asked for one more chance to look at the violin. When the clown opened the case and took out the violin, the expert couldn't believe his eyes: It was an entirely different violin, and, although old, it was in no way the Stradivarius he had seen with his own eyes the previous (admittedly, late) evening. . . . Naturally, he didn't know what had happened, but he clung tenaciously to the hypothesis that the clown had managed to sell the Stradivarius overnight and had replaced it with another violin so no one would be the wiser.

It's perfectly possible that this is, in fact, what happened. Although, right off the bat, this hypothesis strikes me as a little suspect. Really, how could one sell a violin without knowing its price, in one night, when—even if there had been a buyer—all the banks would have been closed? Sure, you could argue that, perhaps, there was already a buyer before the visit by the two experts and that this buyer could have already had the money in hand. Well, then, why did the clown himself invite the experts and not, let's say, the buyer? Why wasn't the buyer present (even in disguise) during the meeting with the experts? A buyer, knowing nothing of violins, would never just trust the seller's words and pay the full price of a priceless instrument. Or perhaps, you'll say, the buyer was in fact in the room that night. It's all quite possible. It's also possible that the buyer was either the expert or the clown himself, or . . . by the way, these "or perhaps" phrases in our story are so abundant that, perhaps, their very abundance puts the whole story in question. A coin can only have two sides, not three or thirty. . . .

It seems to me that, five years later, I have at last found my own explanation for this mysterious story in the line from Verlaine, although this explanation can return neither the clown nor his violin. I think no one sold the violin, nor was it replaced with another. In other words, I believe that it was one and the same violin. Were I Borges, I might say that there was one "ideal" violin, something in the line of the Platonic idea. Not being Borges, I'm inclined to explain what happened as a phenomenon of poetic syntax. The difference between a Stradivarius and an imitation Stradivarius is, of course, huge, but it's not always possible to exactly explain what about this difference bothers us; that is, what the inexplicability really is. In the same way, I am tormented by the inexplicable but obviously real difference between Verlaine's "autumn's violin" and his "autumnal violin," and I am tormented precisely because only one original French violin stands behind the two translations. By the way, we can now ask ourselves whether it is not one and the same violin that reverberates in a concert hall and outside our windows.

Translated by Michael Denner

Longer than a Line, or The "Correspondences" of Hans Viksten

1

In Sweden, they're not much for plein air painting. Not enough light. There's so little light that scholars refer to the situation even when explaining the Swedes' national gloominess and not infrequent, almost bashful, sluggishness.

And that's understandable. You see, Balder, the Scandinavian god of light, had already died in Odin's day.

It seems that a steamy intoxication rules on Zorn's canvases, even as his famous nudes bathe in living rivers.

Fog. Fog and drizzle: lots of tiny, shattering points.

You can't catch hold, cannot grasp.

"Give me a ring, to get me started," the hero will say. "Give me a push and motion, and I will construct a world," Descartes will say. "Give me a point," the artist will say.

A sentence is just as difficult to begin as a painted line. I'd like someone to say the first word, and then I'll proceed, prolong. . . .

"Excuse me. Could you tell me how to get to . . . ?" A typical question in unfamiliar territory. Well, they'll either tell you or show the way. But how to get to the plot—that no one can say.

*   *   *

There is a folkloric way to get in, like a sudden coming into focus:

> A field. In the field, a house. In the house, a room. In the room, a
> cupboard. A cupboard with dishes in it. Silence. And suddenly,
> in the silence, a single white cup shatters.

Viksten's appearance in Swedish art was this sort of an event. A
line, a crack in the paper.

2

The paper is fogged up. A crack in paper is like that opening, cited
by Pushkin, into which only mystics and Don Juans can peer: "I
glimpsed but a slender ankle. . . ."

The fissure of a dash runs between two dates: 1926–1987. They
speak only of the fact that Hans Viksten's life was not long. I will
limit myself to them.

For writing about an artist is just like wandering in a fog. The
objects of a biography, the facts, lose their real distance and scale.
So the unexpectedness of some lamppost in the fog is much more
stunning than the unseen, fog-shrouded city that contains it.

Fog—mist—mysticism.

The only thing that one can catch hold of in a fog is the first de-
tail that crops up.

With the writer, said Chekhov, it's the ink pot.

From the ink pot, then, I'll begin. From the ink pot begins the
line.

There are several plots associated with ink pots, or so Borges might
say. I'll say, "Here are two."

Lenin, in prison, wrote with milk. He fashioned his ink pot out
of bread pulp each day and ate it before the wardens arrived.

Luther, harassed while working on his translation of the Bible,
hurls his ink pot at the devil.

Two lines intrude on the plot. One is like the first contact between lov-
ers' bodies. Passion, appearing cautiously, like a text written in milk.

Hans Viksten was able to love, and he was loved. But more on
that later.

He liked the fact that he resembled Lenin, especially in youth, but with the years that resemblance faded.

But here is another line. It is as if the convolutions of the brain are stretching into a single line. Interrupting that process would push the artist to Lutheranism. Read here: to madness.

Hans Viksten was a madman. There are few madmen in Sweden. Well, of course, there are enough, and even in tiny Lund (where I write these lines), the madhouse occupies a place of honor.

No, I'm speaking of the tempo of his visions, which in a country as practically minded as Sweden, looks like lunacy.

Only madmen can make art in Sweden, and great art there was made precisely by them.

When light is scarce, when little of anything comes in from outside, the only thing left is the light, "the screen," in oneself:

> It is impossible not to feel, to see, to smell one's bankrupt self,
> But one can turn all five innate senses backward—against the
>   circulation.
> And there, fostering one's screen within,
> Splicing oneself forever into a fascicle of spiritual fabric
> With that instrument, where hundreds of Cannes lurk, and you,
>   as if on their leash. . . .
> So that's it, so that's it—look!
> That authentic life connects all
> Who are closed in—rewards, and punishes and shines from
>   inside. . . .

The great eighteenth-century Swede, "the geometrician" Emanuel Swedenborg, who abandoned his renowned scientific activities for the sake of such mystical propensities and, thus, earned the doctors' "paranoid," referred with Swedish sangfroid to angels moving his hand and to Luther(!), whom angels inspired to his crazy translation of the Bible.

Only madmen sense angels.

There are in Sweden soft, milky, smoky-gray angels, like fog, the angels of the madman Erland Kölberg. Probably like those in whose invisible steps cats walk, with purposeful strides unintelligible to us.

There are the great madman Karl Hill's angels, intermittent and melting, like the Cheshire cat.

August Strindberg had a feline face, too.
Strindberg to Viksten is a straight line.

3

Viksten made several drawings devoted to Strindberg. The most powerful of these depicts Strindberg in a prison of voices, of madness. In this drawing, Strindberg resembles Viksten himself. In essence, this Strindberg is another self-portrait.

(Strindberg himself, also a brilliant visual artist, often inscribed his profile within paintings of stormy landscapes. Viksten, his "happy echo," carried this trait to the point of fantastic omnipresence.)

Strindberg was tormented by rats and insects. It seemed to him that someone was always moving the furniture above him. A persecution complex.

Strindberg never emerged from his alcoholic fog. "Alcohol," he wrote, "is my only sedative." Voices tormented him with insomnia.

Strindberg read Luther's Bible and Swedenborg's books, searching them for salvation.

Swedenborg himself lived through something comparable and described the experience in his astonishing *Journal of Dreams.* Characteristic of his struggle, he proposed the annihilation of demons within himself; this was a part of his active spiritual theory.

Strindberg complained: "Only children are capable of seeing angels. We adults see only demons." Thus, despite Swedenborg's thorough descriptions of heaven and hell, Strindberg—in accordance with those very descriptions—concluded that hell begins on earth, that our worldly life *is* hell.

In Swedenborg's terms, which Strindberg borrowed, this epoch in life is called *vastatio,* "the laying waste." Viksten, following both, passed right through it. . . .

> Run my thoughts through? Very well, but with what?
> I might have bared the alcohol sword,
> But unfortunately even that grows dull.

The Viking's wine-sword, turned against oneself—that already has something of Buddhist hari-kari to it. But Valhalla, what a

"wet" word! . . . They gathered there, together with Odin: Stagne-
lius, Lindegren, and many others. . . .

Alcoholism, madness . . . terrifying insect-people, as if from
the visions of Swedenborg and Strindberg, oil-paint relatives of
Goya and Baudelaire, swarming into the brain and drawing it out
into the light:

> And the arachnid nation, mute and gray,
> Moved in with us, beneath our skulls.

This "motif" stayed with Viksten his whole life. It shows up
even in his final pieces, which are devoted to yet another Swede
(the "Swedish Verlaine"), Fröding, also a madman and alcoholic.

"Without wife or home I will soon waste away completely,"
wrote Strindberg.

Strindberg was unfortunate. Viksten had better luck.

4

A person is divisible by one and by three. But one would have to be
a Goethe to save oneself from suicide, having finished off Werther.

Divisibility is scarcely better than primitiveness, and the ten-
dency to bifurcate is already schizophrenia. A person is already
"bifurcated"—into "no" and "yes"—and aggravating that crack
could turn it into an abyss.

(Swedenborg even "calculated" that in every person at least
two good and two evil spirits struggle for influence.)

Be it thus or otherwise, nonetheless, contradictions are insur-
mountable, and, therefore, for the sake of solid footing, in order to
stand, people—and especially those who feel that split sharply—
need a third point. A point of support, a fulcrum.

> . . . and with childish friskiness they rock your tripod.

"You are king—live alone," so said Pushkin. The artist is al-
ways alone. Like Odin. A tripod is more important.

Without a point of support, there can be no motion, no line.
Thus reckoned Swedenborg. In this sense, Oedipus solved the
third part of the Sphinx's riddle incorrectly.

About a husband or wife, one says "My other half." But each is thus simultaneously both alone and bifurcated. . . .

A marriage made in heaven—this is the reflecting angel of the tripartite mirror.

Any happy union is the overcoming of one's personal tendency toward bifurcation, like what happens while contemplating one's face in that triplicating mirror.

Each of its side leaves is exactly half of the center part; they are the "wings of the face." Meanwhile, *the face* is in the center. Only that which is apart from us appears to be whole in our eyes. That is, that at which we are looking. Narcissus's pool, saved from a tragic splash—that is the *closest* other. For a husband, it is his wife; for a wife, her husband. For each of them, his or her own Platonic "half"—this is the center, the middle of the tripartite mirror, without which there is no face, no movement, no flight.

Hans Viksten met Desi and life changed. Flight began, a flight which is still not over in his paintings.

The flight of a lone face. The flight of two, united by a lone pair of wings.

5

There are two primary kinds of human pleasure: the pleasure of the neophyte and the pleasure of constancy.

The first causes amazement. Love and creation are related to this type. But the ability to be amazed (and to amaze) is "erased" with the onset of familiarity, which we might especially call any sort of professionalism. Precisely then, however, the second joy, constancy, opens up, bound by a circle of things and categories that *do not change.*

Let's assume the following: seven pipes a day, every day of the week, one's whole life.

In Russia, this pleasure is unknown, it is a hopelessly foreign feeling, Buddhism. But almost everyone in the West professes this "Buddhism."

When tragedy died in the West, melodrama began a new life in its place. Sentimentalism—that's the way out of tragedism, just like Werther.

But melodrama is also *drama*, only accompanied by *melos*, a peaceful melody. Which, by the way, is how Strindberg dreamed of seeing religion: "Like a peaceful accompaniment to the monotonous music of life."

For Viksten, the melodrama is the chalky (in Russian, *melovaia*) drama of paper, its cracks and lines.

Inasmuch as the pleasure of the neophyte is finite, and the pleasure of constancy verges on "habit" and "boredom," the basis for Western "Buddhism" appears quite simply and naturally. In order not to yield to these afflictions, a person (and artist) is "obligated" not to allow the infantilism in himself to die and to be capable of receiving new joy from observation of the "commonplace." Alterability in the unaltered.

In the kingdom of constancy, objects begin to live their own lives, as in Andersen's fairy tales. In the paintings of another Dane, Wilhelm Hammershøj, all objects have already been carried out: only bare rooms remain, rooms in which windows, walls and doors live out their own lives. To paint only windows and doors one's whole life!

Swedenborg found autonomous life even in the alphabet. As an example of his theory of "correspondences," and as evidence that the soul is separated from the body, he brought up ancient Hebrew, in which vowels are written separately from consonants.

If we develop the notion that alphabets are exponents of national character, we will see that French letters, for example, wear hats, as befits true Parisians, and raise them slightly at rendezvous. Swedish letters also go out for strolls, but with telescopes and binoculars: *å, ä, ö.* . . .

Perspicacity in the fog.

So Viksten referred to himself as a "visionary," not without cause.

The "inner man" of Protestantism, the "inner ear and sight" of Swedenborg, are all nothing more than this condition of perspicacity.

6

There are Pissarro's famous carriages, which seem to move but in fact, stand in place. If one concentrates on an object, it begins to move, as if by telekinesis.

Viksten created an owl which flies, but does not move, as if stopped in the air.

Viksten's owl strangely recalls Baudelaire's "Les Hiboux":

> Sous les ifs noirs qui les abritent,
> Les hiboux se tiennent rangés,
> Ainsi que des dieux étrangers,
> Dardant leur oeil rouge. Ils méditent.
>
> Sans remuer ils se tiendront
> Jusqu'à l'heure mélancolique
> Où, poussant le soleil oblique,
> Les ténèbres s'établiront.
>
> Leur attitude au sage enseigne
> Qu'il faut en ce monde qu'il craigne
> Le tumulte et le mouvement;
>
> L'homme ivre d'une ombre qui passe
> Porte toujours le châtiment
> D'avoir voulu changer de place.

For art, the relationship to motion is definitive. One could say that "Buddhism" in Christian art began with the Impressionists. Claude Monet, for example, is the consummate, complete Buddhist. Having selected one unchanging object, be it the cathedral at Rouen or the pond beside his home, he would submerge it in a "Nirvana" of colors, tracking the transformations of the air. His paintings are a series of "states," "blisses," belonging to a single object. Thus the director, in order to capture on a few minutes of film the birth, efflorescence, and withering of a flower, must patiently wait for these events in real time and only then can compress them into a single moment. Claude Monet's canvases are the ideal animated films, in which anyone who ever took it into his head to do it could, by flipping through them very quickly, see objects begin to move.

Having chosen as motion *only* the movement of light and color, Christian art renounced zealotry and retreated into the Buddhist monastery with its "serene chimes."

It's natural that in the cinema, say, the camera, not the object, moves. An enumeration, a "survey" of these very objects stretches through the entire film, as in Wim Wenders's ingenious *Order of Things*. The film "comes to a boil" only at the very end of the plot.

The absence of "motion," which means something different in each of the arts, leads art to contemplation. (In poetry, for example, "motion" is the development of the image, while "Buddhism" is enumeration, "the catalog" of signs, as, let's say, in works of the majority of Swedish poets.)

For Buddhism, God the Creator and Providence are not necessary. God in Buddhism is immanent in man and nature. Or, as Swedenborg would say, there occurs a "deification of length," that is, of the very line which, according to the great geometer and mystic, is a complete absurdity. For "from nothing comes nothing." To start a line, one must have a *point*. . . . This point, wrote Swedenborg, cannot be seen geometrically, as it is composed of the purest absolute motion. Therefore, it can only be imagined, represented, seen with "the inner eye."
God is "the first point."

Contemplation demands a show, and what is seen demands a tale.
A drawing is closer than anything else to a word, a tale. In it, a gesture is preserved.
Viksten's painting all comes out of drawing, rather than arising only as the self-expression of patches of color. He merely "puts color on" the space between objects, which have an arbitrary scale, as if in a fog. But Viksten's "spiritual visionarianism" is liberty from motion as a decorative effect. For Viksten, motion is the protean characteristic of objects, a transition from one form (or state) to another, the unceasing activeness of the entire painterly system. Swedenborg, whose philosophical system grew out of Ovid's *Metamorphosis*, understood motion in exactly the same way.
For this reason, it is impossible to "displace" Viksten's owl with a glance, as one might with Pissarro's carriages. For the owl flies and does not move *simultaneously*, it is both *from* paradise and already *in* paradise; that is, it is both *from* and *in* the place where the primary "metamorphoses" happen.

This is what Viksten himself wrote about owls in his diary:

Owls are covered with magic. Without owls I would never have
attained color. I've probably drawn several hundred of them in
pen and ink. At times I even feel that I have an owlish counte-
nance. It is quite natural, when a man is so partial to owls, that
something enigmatic happens to him. It seems their strange
magnetic field has influenced the core of my brain. My winged
magi communicate with me by various means. Once, at night, I
heard a chirp and ran out onto the balcony. A tawny owl sat on
the television antenna on our roof.

It is interesting that Swedish visually preserves the enigmatic
but unarguable connection between cats and owls. The Russian
neiasyt' is, in Swedish, *kattuggla,* "cat-owl"—"proteanism," em-
bodied in a single word! "Cat and owl," "swan and albatross," the
"black" and "white" pairs in Baudelaire's bestiary. They interbreed
under Viksten's brush and pen. As they do in the Swedish lan-
guage's biology laboratory, that northern heir to Ovid. As they do
in Swedenborg's Upsala laboratory, and in the alchemy laboratory
of Strindberg.

The fiendishness of owls (in Russian, *besovstvo sov*), the de-
monism of cats, henceforth lose all sense and submit only to one
epic, "angelic" meaning; for in paradise, the conflict of opposition
does not exist, and time itself is indivisible, like Faust's time.

Viksten's owl, in flight and motionless, sounds like "Stay, mo-
ment!"—like the crash of heavenly golden cymbals.

To this we will add that owls, like the Swedish alphabet, are far-
sighted. They are, as it were (in the words of a Russian poet), "fitted
with field glasses," which they use to see only what is not visible to
others. The winged binoculars of God. The triumph of the epic gaze
from outside into creation.

After the artist's death, while Desi Viksten was working on her hus-
band's diaries (from which the passage on owls is taken), an "owl-
cat" suddenly landed on the roof of the workshop. In broad daylight
and in Stockholm—you are forced, willy-nilly, to ask, was it from
there? . . .

7

Viksten was often called "the Swedish Matisse." Matisse illustrated Baudelaire.

(Before me lie two portraits of Baudelaire, one by Matisse and one by Rodin. The first is a typical bourgeois, the second—the Etruscan head of an idiot.)

Baudelaire wrote his famous sonnet "Correspondences" inspired by Swedenborg, and in general he used the word "hieroglyph" as Swedenborg used and understood it: as *the cryptography of the spirit.*

Until Champollion deciphered them in the nineteenth century, Egyptian hieroglyphs were also understood this way. In the eighteenth century, Swedenborg saw in them the unresolved wisdom of God, expressed in a sign. His "hermeneutics," a multivolume deciphering of the Bible, grew into a spiritual theory and then into mystical visionarianism. "Hermeneutics" also lies at the foundation of Luther's Reformation.

But—so thought Swedenborg—precisely poets, more than others, understand (or rather feel, see "with the inner eye") the original thought contained in the hieroglyphs of the Creator.

Artists love poets.

Viksten the artist loved the poet in himself. He usually "accompanied" his graphic visions with verses. This without question bespeaks his lofty "infantilism": "Otherwise, they just won't understand." You see, it's characteristic of infantilism to relate to others as if they were children, what the Russian poet called "spending a little time and playing with the people."

One often encounters the content-laden Swedenborgian term "cipher" in Viksten's verse, along with an almost childish craving to peep into God's keyhole!

> A boot sole
> Punches a keyhole in the earth
> But there's no key to unlock it.

A powerful metaphor for human powerlessness!

But on that side of "the door," according to Swedenborg, our spiritual substances flow into one Great Being, which is the "visualization" of God's thought, the "materialization" of his unchanging order. The Great Being is constantly taking shape from newly arrived spirits and their displacements. Spirits forever seek their uniquely proper place in this body. Thus, the Great Being corresponds only with the unique and unchangeable fixed "point" in the universe—God.

Where, then, is paradise to be found? In that place where all contradictions are finally "canceled"? Once, writes Swedenborg, angels led him into the heavenly garden, which was situated "just above the right eye" of the Great Being. Truly, that is where a visionary's paradise ought to be!

"The lock," according to Swedenborg, opens with the help of "correspondences." Everything *here* somehow corresponds to what is *there*, and one need only be able to see that.

In both painting and verse, Hans Viksten wrote his own "Baudelairian sonnet" on Swedenborg's theme. He "read" the metonym of "correspondences" like a splendid metaphor, and his "flights" are a kind of realization of that trope. This is how it happens in words:

> The sun is our postman,
> The cloud, a mystery-bearing package,
> The tree of life postmarks
> The stamps of bodies.
> We fly away from earth
> Toward our postal existence.

Correspondences—letters—flight . . . beautiful reading!

At the beginning of his career, Swedenborg published several volumes of the journal *Daedalus*, in which he publicly proposed a project, unheard of in the eighteenth century, for a motorless flying machine, similar to the contemporary glider. He presented the project to Charles XII, not hoping, however, that it would be realized.

Having realized the metaphor of "correspondences," Viksten's "Daedaluses" flew fearlessly toward that Sun which does not melt wings.

8

Of course, Hans Viksten in no way illustrated Swedenborg. But the law of correspondences is an active law, and uncovered "inner vision" is capable of seeing the very same things. Here, I am sure, the "general Swedish" nature of Viksten, Strindberg, and Swedenborg is especially important.

Fog. Perspicacity. The ability to see in a line.

But Viksten painted magically: A line begins completely unexpectedly (from somewhere in a corner), and, breaking up, forms itself into a leaf. . . . The process is like the words of the servant directed toward Pushkin's Don Juan:

> Our imagination
> Will complete the drawing in an instant;
> It is more adroit than an artist,
> It's all the same, no matter what you start from,
> Be it the brow, or the feet. . . .

Viksten always unerringly selected that "point" from which a line begins, his graphical phrase. The absolute feeling of composition (of God . . .), which is, clearly, the only "correspondence" to happiness.

I have seen several films about "the Swedish Matisse," and was always reminded of a film about Matisse himself, in which the *maître* is also filmed at work.

He stands before the easel in costume, in a white shirt and tie, palette in hand. Like the overplump director of a bank. "Make your deposits, gentlemen!"

In life, Viksten was famous, but he never managed to get any special "deposits."

9

Hans Viksten died in great pain. Of cancer. But in endless hospitals, he drew, constantly (to the last day), fixing every moment of his pain and liberation.

The Buddhism of death.

*   *   *

His final drawing portrays fishing. Like an evangelical parable. His
father, hauling in the net. Hans, rowing toward the shore. Desi, sit-
ting in the boat—the three of them. . . .

Hans Viksten departed quietly, like a letter dropped in a postbox,
with Desi leaning over her husband, like an Italian fresco.

Swedenborg described the moment of death with the instanta-
neousness of Michelangelo's gravestones or El Greco's murals. Two
angels sit beside the heart of the dying person, two more at the head
of the bed. At the moment of death, the angels gather and preserve
the man's thoughts. These angels remain with the soul until it
reaches the shore of eternal life.

When they have completed their mission, their place is taken
by spiritual angels, who open up the soul's inner vision. To this
point, the soul has experienced liberation only intellectually. Now
the soul feels it. Each spirit gravitates toward that circle of spirits
which shares its thoughts and feelings as they were formed during
earthly life. So long as a spirit does not find its true, final place in
the Great Being, it will, for some "time," lead a life corresponding
exactly to its life on earth. According to the doctrine of "correspon-
dences," the spiritual territory is a copy of the terrestrial. This
"identity" is so exact, Swedenborg holds, that many "newly de-
ceased" don't even realize that they've died. . . .

Everything is exactly the same, but everything is shrouded in a
fog which does not dissipate. Again, and for ever, fog.

I believe that, even now, Hans Viksten continues to do what he al-
ways did: to see in a line.

But the main thing, Swedenborg warns, is to bury a man properly.

Hans Viksten was buried properly. His grave lies not far from that
of August Strindberg.

Lund, October 1991–April 1992

Translated by Peter Thomas

Hieroglyphs of Swedish Poetry

In the eighteenth century, the great Swedish writer-mystic Emanuel Swedenborg came out with a theory of correspondences, according to which our world and everything in it are hieroglyphs of another world, and—precisely through these hieroglyphs—it is possible to recognize and even to see that other world.

For me, Swedish poetry is, in many respects, the hieroglyph of a greater world which may be called Swedish psychology.

Much in Swedish poetry can, therefore, seem strange to the foreign reader, as can the Swedish national psychology itself, when he bumps into it.

What do we know about Scandinavia? Almost nothing. Yes, we know that Sweden, after Finland, is the closest Western country to the Russian border, although the Swedes themselves don't consider Sweden the West. They are the North. And if we add to that that, for Swedes, Sweden is by no means Europe (Europe begins on the continent), then it turns out that everything we know about Sweden is a bit off. But can one's knowledge of her be right on? I don't know. The more I find out about Sweden, the more the question of understanding remains an open one. Like the eyes of a blind man. But if

Greece exists through Homer's eyes, then why can't Sweden be seen through a blind man's?

True, even if our eyes are open, Sweden is a closed country. She is particular, as the Swedes hold, and aloof, even in geographic terms. Although, the Swedes invest no messianic sense in the word "particular." Quite the opposite. If, for example, I say, "This is a prominent man," they won't quite understand me, for a man is not a maxillary, like that of famous Swedish Hollywood actor Max von Sydow, that he might jut out like a *promontory*.

By "particular," Swedes imply only their aloofness, independence, self-sufficiency. Hence—Swedish neutrality in politics; hence, also—the notorious Swedish insularity.

The primary Swedish virtues are "modesty," simplicity, democratism, all instilled in Swedes not least by Lutheran morality and the conviction that God judges a person not according to deeds, that is, not by what he did, wrote, and so on, in this life, but according to what he kept in his heart.

For a long time (during which she was one of the most powerful states in Europe), Sweden remained an agricultural country. There were few cities, and peasant farmsteads stood at a great distance from each other. People would go to the city two times a year, before Christmas and Easter, and as almost everything had to be made from scratch, little time remained for conversation. Hence, the rather vast diapason of self-expression. Many Swedish poets, for example, are also artists and musicians. For this reason, nature is to the Swede that with which he has lived privately for centuries. Even the design of the Swedish governmental system was dictated by nature. Look at the sky on a sunny day, and you will see the Swedish flag just the way it appeared—a sign on a banner—to one of the Swedish monarchs. Even the Swedish coat of arms—three golden crowns on a blue field—can be found in the guise of yellow lilies on a provincial Swedish pond.

Linnaeus lives in almost every Swede; almost all Swedes are hereditary ornithologists. And if, say, the Russian, Frenchman, or Italian spends his free time in the theater, then the Swede will almost certainly prefer field to opera glasses, so as to observe what is far more interesting for him—the premiere of the cranes' mating dance.

Therefore, when explaining themselves with signs from their natural world, Swedish poets, who are understandable to Swedes, are pretty much absolute Masons for outsiders. But no matter what sort of fairy-tale monsters we might suspect behind this or that word, that "buzzard" simply shows itself to be a "hawk," because Swedes never write about rare exotic plants or animals. On the contrary. Even for their symbol of faith the Swedes will choose some bird like, say, a sparrow, and it seems to me that exactly in the most humble of birds the Swedish language overheard its own measured twittering. The Danes, in contrast to the Swedes, give clear preference to crows and eagles. Their language is bellicose, like cawing above the field of a long finished battle. . . .

Sweden is often called the Northern Japan. Even leaving aside the Swedish "economic miracle," there is a grain of truth in this nickname. Although Swedes are (for the most part) Protestants, at base they are Buddhists. And not merely because the contemplation of birds and flowers is the greatest relaxation for Swedes. The tempo of the Japanese tea ceremony is the normal tempo of Swedish thoroughness, especially in conversation.

The main thing in a Swedish conversation is to endure the pause. We blurt out words; we say a lot and say it chaotically. Swedes say little, and probably for that reason—in accordance with the logic of their character—the language itself possesses the ability to contain many words within one. Not squandering words but, rather, gathering them, words against word, kernel against kernel, into one. For after humility, the main characteristic of Swedes is considered to be thrift.

Translators from English often complain that English words are shorter than Russian words. I can console them: Swedish words are many times longer. The anthological "Swede—Russian—Stab—Cleave—Slice" (from Pushkin's poem "Poltava") could with some effort be gathered into one *loooonnnng* Swedish word, an impossibility in Russian.

Although even Gogol, not without minding the language, wrote that "suddenly it became visible in all corners of the earth," and the Poltavian Gnedich ingeniously equipped his translation of the *Iliad* with various "mighty-masterly" and "terrible howling" words, this means of word formation did not take root. For the Russian, language is metaphorical, while for the Swede it is metonymical. In contrast to the unspoiled nature of the Swedish peasant, the Swedish language does not sow but, rather, immediately reaps.

The Swedish character is reflected not only in morphology, but also in syntax. Distinct from the grammatical certainty of "I don't want," "I don't like," the Swedish negation, following the verb, sounds like uncertainty in the emotions and feelings themselves or like humility or a desire not to offend immediately: "I want not," "I like not," "I know not."

All these qualities are characteristic of Swedish poetry as well: sentimentality, which one might take (not knowing) for infantilism; the absence of muscular movement in the face and exterior humility, which one might take for sullenness; a thoroughness most easily interpreted as sluggishness; and so forth.

In splendid Protestant cathedrals there is no ornamentation; their walls are practically bare. In Swedish poetry there is no ornamentation either. Everything has been cleared away, even end rhyme, leaving only the faith that poetry is still there. Rhyme does occur in Swedish poetry, however; it's just like watercolors. Like Gioconda's smile.

Since Sweden has suffered no cataclysm for some time now, and even the very stones here seem polished by the centuries, Swedish culture has been immersed in such a profound continuum, in such a historical "Nirvana," that Russians and Americans, raised on eschatology, always feel like shaking or shouting her awake, like a prince waking a sleeping beauty. Swedish culture is, however, in no way asleep—she is simply privy to different plans and their resolutions, plans for the time being unknown to most other cultures.

Simply put, the muscle of tragedy withered and has fused with the face. The veins don't protrude with each pulse, as they do on race horses; rather, the pulse beats, as it does in humans, and if it beats intermittently, then the person is dying.

In Sweden, as everywhere, there is a lot of stress, but stresses don't show on the surface, and a man often dies not wanting to show that things are going badly for him. But that's not tragedy; it's melodrama. A completely different genre.

For that very reason, there is little pathos and no "exoticism" in Swedish poetry. Verses are distributed in even layers, like snow falling on a flat surface, and that is perhaps the only "sign" that they were written in the exotic north of Europe.

Alexander Blok wrote of Chinese poetry that "it somehow demands an effort of those who would enjoy it," a typically Russian point of view and one wholly applicable to the apprehension of Swedish poetry.

If one were to divide poetry into that of "exits" (of ecstasy, of glossolalia) and that of "entrances" (of meditations on every sign, which uncover an entryway into the whole), then Russian poetry shows itself more often than not to be the poetry of "exits," and Swedish poetry the poetry of "entrances."

The great Danish writer Hans Christian Andersen attempted to cut everything out of paper, like the spirit which, having created Scandinavia, cut out of blue paper the numberless islands and islets called by the Swedish Adam (in a period of blissful glossolalia) fjords. It is as if Swedish poets cut out that which has already been named and glue it onto the page: Look, and if you are able, enjoy.

Peasant Sweden, it seems, has never died in Swedish poetry, where words find themselves as far from one another as dwellings, and these gaps are at times even polygraphically marked. "Distant ideas" are not bound by the nautical knot of metaphor. Gravitating toward metonym, Swedish poetry runs up (quite frequently) against the sign, which means so much that, for an outsider, it means almost nothing. Hence, there prevails an absolutely different relation to the "detail" and, therefore, to the "composition."

There exists a Chekhovian law about the gun which must fire if it is hanging above the mantel. With regard to Swedish poetry, this law is almost never in effect. Word-signs in no way cooperating with one another are pinned to the page like butterflies, and almost every Swedish poet, like a good collector, considers simply having them in the text to be indispensable. Quite possibly this trait derives from Strindberg, who didn't much like glancing back at lists of characters he had himself placed at the beginnings of plays and who sometimes introduced personages not appearing on those lists while forgetting to "activate" the characters that had been mentioned.

Translated by Peter Thomas

Stagnelius's Mustache

for Hans Rausing

1

Many Americans, I believe, are familiar with the milk advertisements of their luminaries, including—if I am not mistaken—the president himself, with a milk mustache: "rich in calcium." Mustache or no mustache, while watching somebody like Larry King on TV, we start wondering about his milk barber and whether we still have some of it left in the refrigerator.

Commercials, for better or worse, belong to the associative part of our brain, often mixed up with the more precious memories—like, for example, a random verse into which we run with the frequency of any contingency, poetry included. Probably, this is not completely correct, because the best (or the worst) that can be said about the human brain is that it doesn't stop scanning itself, and thus everything that is presumably forgotten, like that old verse, or that which wants to become it, like many a contagious commercial, is nevertheless only an exchange of two bottom lines. In this case, contingency is not an accident but an inescapability of life: a line in a supermarket on a Saturday morning with us waiting in it to finally pay for, say, milk. Sooner or later, it—this line—comes to us, and this is inevitable.

Likewise, the associations which pop up in our mind are, in fact, the result of the continuity of another line—of the lost, forgotten, and inert. Associations, in truth, are nothing but fishing in Lethe from this side of the shore, because on the opposite bank even the Apostles forget that they are fishermen. (See section 10.) Still, drink your milk and don't drink from Lethe!

2

The diffuseness of the aforesaid is due to the odd chain (line) of associations, at which I caught myself while meditating, for the nth time, over the milk-mustache advertisement in one more American magazine. I remembered myself in Moscow in the seventies, or, more exactly, I remembered patiently standing in a chronic queue, moving—very slowly—from the street to a grocery store. (Groceries were many, but always half empty and never half full.) After an hour or so, you had a good chance to get yourself out with, at least, a packet of milk. A packet, indeed, for in those days milk was on sale in paper pyramids, in which, so studies say, liquids, like Pharaohs, defend themselves better against bacteria. When cutting off the pyramid's top at home and then squeezing its corpus, you were presented with another association—of some mini-volcano—and could have been easily taking your milk for the latter's heavy smoke.

Flashbacks, as in Sergei Eisenstein's banned sequence in *Ivan the Terrible,* are often conveyed in smoke, because you never know how far your memory will be taken by the wind. Almost directly from the Moscow milk queue it took me to the Swedish city of Lund. There, in the very first supermarket, I discovered that my favorite milk pyramids were no more, that they were replaced with the parallelepipeds, also preserving various juices. (In Russia, we only knew canned ones, from India.) Moreover, this provision trigonometry also came from Lund, or, more exactly, from Tetra-Pak's headquarters in one of this city's not innumerable streets.

Now, when thinking about milk packing, I cannot resist the definition of "poetry" as a well-packed Milky Way. In fact, there is no drastic difference between packing liquids and packing lines. Although Boris Pasternak once likened a poem's stanza to a casket containing Sleeping Beauty, I would rather liken it to a pyramid or a parallelepiped. Yet, lines wrapped up in parallelepipeds are far too many (people call them quatrains), while those in pyramids— with the probably far-fetched exception of Dylan Thomas's "Vision and Prayer"—are, alas, nonexistent.

Still, pyramids in poetry—to the credit of Osip Mandelstam, who concatenated poetry with cult edifices—as well as Cheops's pyramid are as much a formal intrigue as are the pyramids of milk, save that the latter, designed by a cult of American luminaries, would probably be of a more relevant appearance in the desert. Lund—this former lactose Gaza in its transition to becoming a Manhattan (skyscrapers are in love with parallelepipeds)—links me to Erik Stagnelius.

3

Who was he? A Swede, a poet.

What do sand and snow have in common? Or, more exactly, what do the distant grounds covered by sand or snow have in common? I would say, the subject of history, or rather the alien (direct or angular) attempts to change its course. Both, sand and snow, make these attempts difficult, if not futile. Although hardly less gifted a commander than General Schwarzkopf, the Roman Marcus Crassus got stuck in the Parthian, now Iranian, desert and lost his life and legions. Had Crassus had modern weapons, the results might or might not have been different; Germans, with tanks, didn't make it—neither through the yellowness of Egypt nor the whiteness of Russia. Napoleon tried both and was similarly foiled.

Unlike Crassus or Napoleon, poets don't suffer the desert's hostility because they already are, so to speak, genetically acquitted deserters from—what people think of as—normal life: This little part of the deal poets simply owe to their line of work. In a sense, they are "professional" hermits living in a synthetic and figurative desert, which, as good as any, remains rich in fata morgana and erotic traps, that is, in mirages and images. In order to assign this desert to themselves—and to feel secure that poetry won't abandon them—poets quite often desert profitable careers and even their families: everything that could put their duty in jeopardy.

Half-boisterous, half-demonic creature, sort of a hybrid of Kipling's Mowgli and of Beelzebub, such was the poet's portrait in romanticism. Nowadays, nobody takes this hackneyed portrayal seriously, with the exception, perhaps, of a few souls still faithful to this sentimental drivel. But it is a powerful portrait. Wilderness is in the poet's genes, and this is his evil jinn, too, whom he'd better keep under a cork. Even then, a poet, to the great displeasure of his nearest and dearest, often conducts himself as a "monster," whether he wants to or not, because everything in him works on just one mission: surpassing time. In the *Exegi monumentum,* Horace proudly announced that his works will "surpass" even— yes!—"Egypt's pyramids." (See final section.)

No wonder that the purposes of a poet and of a pyramid are actually similar. Each pyramid is an architectonic celebration of a Pharaoh's life; whether his life was placid or paltry, whether he died a youngster, the size of a pyramid can tell it otherwise, because what is ocular, and presumably timeless, negates the reliability of history, that is, of human memory. To put it bluntly, we wouldn't even remember the looks of our dead, let alone their voices, were not their photos kept in a scrapbook. From a photograph, even a jerk, who is—and we say, fortunately—already dead, is nonetheless given a chance at posthumous betterment. For an eye is more persuasive than some factual remembering, which it often cheats. That is why poets are concerned with their works more than with their often sloppy behavior.

Because poetry is relatively easy to memorize and even easier to forget, our memory cannot be truly trusted; and since poetry, to which we all like to listen, has become an optic art, it, too, requires from its messengers not just a spoken declaration of loyalty but some palpable confirmation as well. In the poet's pyramid, his works are bricks. Even if others prefer them to be firewood. Pyramids of burning books, however, celebrate the hot content inside their bindings, and not their "architects."

Poets slave for their Muse, like the Jews did for the Pharaohs. "All poets are Jews," Marina Tsvetaeva once wrote. She meant among other things that poets—like Jews—have a long history of being disdained and existing as outcasts, so it probably won't be a strained interpretation if I say that poets are not so much a profession as a nationality. Without even leaving the place of their "Egypt," they nevertheless are a nation of wanderers in some desert. Wanderers but not necessarily survivors.

4

Islands are just another version of deserts. Erik Johan Stagnelius was born (in 1793) on the Swedish island of Öland. While a boy, he—like all children—loved the stones and sand of the shore. He probably even compared himself to Jesus in the desert, of which the sea before his eyes was an extension. (Correspondingly, the heat of the desert transforms its horizon into a liquid.)

Why—exactly—to Jesus? Erik's father was a reverend, and bringing his son's life into alignment with the life of Christ, just in order to perfect it, would have been an expected and welcomed effort from his son's side. Moreover, later in Erik's life dryness, childhood remained its single oasis, full of scents and roses, and precisely Jesus became its guardian and gardener.

"Rich in romanticism" can be, of course, said about any rose garden. Poets and nightingales cannot at all resist its scent harmony. But what about its many thorns?

5

Scent and thorns. Harmony and, yes, harm. Are they just an onus of some morphological solitaire? Doesn't it sometimes happen that precisely that which makes you now reverberate (oh, this rose and that nightingale!) hurts your future ear the most? Harmony is perilous, or, as Rilke might have put it, *ist schrecklich*. Names belong to the same category, so to speak. For us, their bearers, names intend consolation, guardianship; they even symbolize some kind of a metaphysical placenta, for they are its extension into our existence: We are born into our names. Names—for the bearers—often become carriers, however, because names *are* contagious.

The most aggressively antipositivist and thus poetic of what has been written on this matter is probably the book *Names* (1926) by Father Pavel Florensky, not just a religious philosopher but a mathematician, too, and—though it merely touches upon the subject of how writers take their own names—I, also a writer, still don't want my claims to be unfounded. I will quote, first, about how and why names happen to be crucial for the poet's mind. "Sometimes," writes the Russian metaphysician,

> the formation of a human type around the name goes on not entirely consciously, and a poet, leaning on his intuitively given name, does not himself fully know how precious it is to him. Only in the case of some unspecified inevitability of parting from it, the indispensability of this very name—as a center point and heart of the entire *Ding*—would have been discovered. However, we should not overstate this unconsciousness of a poet: It is not a rule. In many cases, inspiration knows what it does; it is not just a process of inevitability,—it is aware of this very inevitability. The latter concerns—and probably it is the only case when this is truly relevant—names. And writers have often pointed to this function of a name—of a keystone of an arch.

Second—and this is crucial—Florensky looks upon a poet's name as the superior source of his or her later creativity. And hence he himself sounds almost like a poet, that is, a bit bathetic.

> The name is a thinnest possible slice of flesh, by which our spiritual essence manifests itself. . . . Our own name is an interior concentrate of all other names; it manifests itself in just one word, though it draws the energies of a person into full circle. . . . Oeuvre . . . , because it is born from/by the author and has not just been mechanically put together, it leans on some primary intuition and serves as its embodiment. Where exactly, I ask, has this intuition then been struck? In that place, where the lightning of imagination strikes the entire verbal organism. The place around which this organism conceives. Because this very first cell *should* be verbal; whatever process of a pre-verbal ripening might have been, at a certain point it finally becomes worded, and therefore some primal verbal occurrence does exist. There is no doubt: In literary creation names are categories of self-cognition, because in the creative imagination they have the power of personal forms.

And now—my final quotation from Florensky's work. "A name," he writes, is the face, the personality, and this or that name is a person of this or that typical cast of mind. Not only to a fairy-tale hero, but also to a real man, his name either betokens or delivers his character, his spiritual and physical features—to his *destiny*.

6

And now imagine the same Swedish boy, Erik, who walks along the seashore. "Stag-ne-li-us"—he rinses his mouth with the last name's syllables, and to him they feel exactly like Demosthenes' correctional pebbles. This kind of early-life-morning rinsing cleansed his—not far off!—unique diction a lot. But why?

Shakespeare's Juliet, when meditating upon Romeo's name, recalled a rose. In this, her association was of a nightingale in a rose garden. In the case of Stagnelius, his meditation on his name would probably have been similar to Romeo's own perception of his name, if we only had a chance to speak with this character about how his name sounded to him. For both, Romeo and Stagnelius, were poets—remember the former writing sonnets at dawn?—and sound is poetry's major engine: Any truly poetic ear—like that of a doe—always oscillates slightly. Because both, Stagnelius and Romeo, are, yes, *Romans:* Rome is their names' phonetic, so to speak, blood. And because the first sounds, to recall Florensky, to which future poets listen attentively are their own names.

This is not the right place to discuss how Roman was the Shakespearean Romeo. I think that his entire conduct was. But the name Stagnelius—with its *us* at the end—should indeed have sounded premonitory to the young ear: "Am I from the same line of *us*es as all those greatest: Julius, Catullus, Ovidius, Horatius, Propertius, and so on?" (No wonder, then, that Stagnelius's first favorites in poetry were exactly those Romans, whom—Propertius and Horatius—he brilliantly translated later.) "And how about Jesus himself, after all?"

Imagine—for the last time—this phonetically precocious boy who asks himself all these crazy questions. Imagine—in order to understand not just his later life but also ourselves, that is, *us*.

7

This English "us" is here on purpose, of course: Our language per se reacts to Latin, that is, involves its own linguistic *associational* drive. Quite at random, I take from my bookshelf *The Complete Works of Horace,* published in 1938. In the introduction—on its first page—I read: "This year marks the two-thousandth year of the birth of Quint*us* Horati*us* Flacc*us*. . . . He is essentially the poet of all of *us*. . . . The reign of August*us* was the culmination of a century of heart-breaking civil war, of tumultuo*us* political struggles . . . ," and so on, and so on.

That which is still noteworthy in this generally unnecessary excerpt from another book or introduction is the sureness with which even some boring and unpoetic writing *on* Latin subjects inevitably entails in English all its various *us*es. Even an unpoetic linguistic reaction to Latin is justified. And how about something more "poetic," such as, for example, the two "empires"—of Rome and the U.S.? Huh?

Anyhow, if in English its numerous *o-us-es* suffixes are drawn from Latin, they did not become equally familiar in Swedish, at least in their frequency. So a word such as "Stagnelius" would be really opprobrious if used as, say, an adjective. If, however, a Swede hears it, he or she becomes immediately attracted to the word's sound because of its Latin glockenspiel, its strangeness and yet zest. "Stagnelius" does sound Roman in Swedish. It also sounds like something very medieval: either a Sorbonnique student or a poet of the Thirty Years' War walking with a torch in the plague-stricken streets of Europe. Like, I presume, François Villon (143?–46?) or Andreas Gryphius (1616–64). As to the former (even the French are not still sure how his name should sound: "Viyon" or "Vilon"), his *l'enfant terrible* kind of life, as well as its dates, is still a big question mark. The latter—a German poet writing in Latin—remains a baroque bum.

Stagnelius as a person somehow featured both, but—as a poet—rigorously followed his *us*-vector. Its full direction I'll draw a bit later. Because drawings often start from the low corner of paper or from that invisible tip or point about which only the artist's intuition knows. And what is more comparable to a drawing in literature than the essay genre?

8

To my Russian ear, "Stagnelius" sounds like mustache, because in my native language *us* means exactly that. Despite the fact that the Romans were usually well shaved, their language in Russian has a bushy face. But when I heard Stagnelius's name for the first time, I imagined its bearer to be a late-Latin poet who should have looked like somebody in between, say, Stéphane Mallarmé and Salvador Dalí. Of the former—long mustache, its ends always down: they recall a very thin brush for India ink—a mag*us* working on the single book, the single hieroglyph, of his life; the monotono*us*ness of this life, its *tristesse*. Of the latter—long brave mustache, always up: brushes erect while anticipating with pleasure their palette—his furio*us* life. I thought about Stagnelius as their "middle," because, I repeat, I didn't know anything about his life or work; because in the word "Stagnelius" I heard—with my Russian ear—its Latin "unshavenness" and—with my English one—its "stagnation."

Mallarmé + Dalí = Stagnelius. This would be my graffiti on the walls of the St. Maria Church in Stockholm, the place where he is buried. This inscription of mine (of course, imaginable) would be there instead of the usual I + You = Love, because I was already in love with Erik Johan Stagnelius. And because, although I have crossed—and probably a hundred times—its churchyard (it was a smart shortcut to the apartment of my Stockholm friends), I didn't even have the slightest idea that that very church gave a final roof to my "Latin" Swede.

Moreover, precisely at the exit from the churchyard, I finally saw—in the window of a used-book store—*Samlade skrifter* of Stagnelius. They were in five volumes, not cheap but very beautiful: black covers with ancient figures. Like simultaneously an obituary and a Greek vase. Just another "sum." An urn.

Yes, my "ancient" Swede died young: twenty-nine years old (in 1823). And when I—and, again, finally—saw his portrait, his was a face without any real mustache: just peach fuzz. His was, however, exactly the face for a milk advertisement, because in my native language we usually say about people his age "the milk still hasn't dried on his lips," which is the Russian translation of "wet behind the ears."

Though I write this in English, I think Russian + American = milk mustache of Stagnelius.

9

In his essay on Auden, "To Please a Shadow," Joseph Brodsky writes: "I began to wonder whether one form of art was capable of depicting another, whether the visual could apprehend the semantic." In my Stagnelius case, both visual and semantic met each other quite conveniently: He happened to be exactly that kind of a poet whose "linguistic" face his name had promised me.

Yes, Stagnelius's was a stagnating life: From a very happy childhood on a beach, it eventually came to many nasty conclusions. That is why he was afraid of growing up. Already a morning nomad of his childhood dunes, for the rest of his short life he felt the freezing chill of a desert at night. That's why he was an alcoholic. That's why—according to his personal poetic mythology— night on earth is infinite and sickening, while day is that which warms heaven and thus is also endless but gracious. (Upon the details of this mythology I'll touch soon.)

Nothing is as vulgar as the concept of a poet's life appearing to be fundamentally dramatic and hence traumatic. Such a concept is a cliché, kitsch. And it stinks, like kitchen garbage. Stagnelius, however, *was* a romantic-era poet and persona. This meant that living with a constant cloud over one's head should be taken as the only normal weather, the one and only appropriate lifestyle.

Romantic "sufferings" start from biting one's fingernails. They are called "unrequited love." In showing themselves, these feelings are nevertheless a young horse's gait, *l'allure*. Stagnelius had already started as a thoroughbred, well-drilled trotter clattering with Swedish hexameters and Ovidius's elegiac couplets. (The latter, I quote from my shabby *Webster's Dictionary*, "consists of two dactylic hexameter lines, the second of which lacks the arses in the third and sixth feet.") So Stagnelius clattered against the cobblestones of his "unrequited loves," Constance Magnet and Fredrique Almgren (a fifteen-year-old girl!), whom Stagnelius called by just one name: Amanda.

> Fåfängt, Amanda, min sång du försmår, mitt brinnande hjärta,
> fåfängt skilja oss åt alper och brusande hav,
> mild som en ängel ändå omsvävar du evigt min tanke,
> flicka, min ömma brud är du i drömmen ändå.

Try to read it aloud (in Swedish, words are pronounced as they are written), and you'll hear the hexameter's gait, which my very rough translation can't convey.

> Vainly, Amanda, my song you dismiss, my burning heart,
> vainly separate us alps and heaving sea,
> gentle like an angel nevertheless you hover around my thought,
> girl, my loving bride you are in dream nevertheless.

Stagnelius's Amanda was, of course, an ordinary poetic trick of the time. Thus, for example, the French preromantic Evariste Parny, whose "unrequited love" was called Esther, invented a special poetic name for her—Eleanore—and, of course, everybody tried to guess just who this *elle* was in reality. Does it really matter? And even if it does, aren't those people just deaf? Doesn't Eleanore in general sound like a name that has been derived exactly from *elle*, a generic "she"?

Stagnelius's Amanda also comes, certainly, from French *âme*, the "soul," which—in its turn—comes from Latin *anima*. Moreover, precisely Anima later becomes a major character in Stagnelius's gloomy mythology.

10

At the same time, the Amanda of Stagnelius comes—also most certainly—from two Swedish words: *anda*, which means "breath" and "atmosphere," and *ande*, which means "spirit" or "ghost." In short, "Amanda" means many ethereal things and even philosophical concepts; she sounds both Platonic and sepulchral. Hence, the entire Stagnelius mythology is one of both hope and despair. But for now—about the "landscape" of this kind of mythology.

We already know that the future poet was born by the seaside. Let us imagine now a small Swedish town, built up by the shore and feeding itself from the sea. Let us imagine its small houses, which remind us of salt and pepper shakers. Not some chessboard figures, but salt and pepper shakers, without which even the threatening hand of the Sistine Chapel would not have been able to preside as chef over this landscape. These houses are part of the generally flavorless panorama, but they add taste to it. And because of all this, one understands that, if God exists, then he is not like some Bobby Fischer, who moves his figures—that is, us—with *far-sighted* plans in mind, but is rather a fisherman, like those who live in that small town and survive on what they get from the water *to-day*. Not for nothing were the Apostles initially fishermen, too.

Weekday God. Weekday life, when all men are at sea and their women wait for them at home. Empty shore, empty cobblestone streets.

Stagnelius's childhood: The sky is always blue and friendly.

The rest of Stagnelius's life: The sky turns to gray from blue. Then—even grayer. Finally, it becomes raven black, and there is that feeling in the air when anxiety pastes itself onto an otherwise peaceful soul. From then on, the soul is always prepared for the worst; the blue sky has fled from the earth, though it exists somewhere and far away. Like God. Or, probably, he is only as far away as those men at sea, which was also blue but has turned gray. And here, along the shore, walks Anima, or Psyche, the soul, the woman, who lost her blue sky, him, Jesus; who waits for him to come back and embrace her. As does the fisherman's wife when her husband—all pale from rolling and pitching—at last returns home. But he is not coming back. And she, Anima, even already agrees that he won't, and that he is in heaven (Stagnelius calls it his own term—*Saron*).

> Ur Kyrkans modersarmar jagad,
> Av bleka minnen blott ledsagad,
> Går Psyche, höljd i sorgens flor,
> På stränderna, där döden bor.
>
> Än ses hon mot Olympen häva
> Sin blick, där vemodstårar bäva;
> Än slår hon, tynande och matt,
> Den långsamt ned till jordens natt.
>
> Av rosor kransad sitter kvällen
> I purpurdräkt på västra fjällen.
> Ett återsken av glädjens land
> Ser själens öga i dess brand. . . .
>   (*Brudgummen*, 1819?)

> Exiled from the Church's motherly arms,
> Accompanied only by dim recollections,
> Went Psyche, wearing a mourning crape,
> Along the beaches, where death lives.

Still, she casts toward Olympus
Her glance, in which the tears of sorrow tremble;
Still, casts she, unwell and weak,
Her eyes slowly down onto the earthly night.

Crowned with the roses sits the evening
In the purple cloth on the west bank.
A reflection of the land of merriment
Sees the soul's eye in this fire.
                    (*Bridegroom*, 1819?)

Stagnelius's Anima behaves exactly like the same fisherman's
wife, who *feels* that her husband has been lost at sea and only
hopes that he—if already dead—managed to get to heaven. Or,
perhaps, he got to some better country, and then she knows—it
would take time for him to return. Or, maybe, he even found some-
body else there. And she, unfortunately, should eventually re-
marry, too. (In Stagnelius, Anima already had: Her new husband's
name is Demiurge.) Or, if he hadn't, hopes she, then he would have
at least sent her some small token which says that he still remem-
bers and cares. In the case of Stagnelius's Anima, she craves a
quick "divorce" from Demiurge, and her First Love's token of love
and responsibility becomes, of course, a romantic and mystical
rose from Eden's garden.

. . . En underblomma där han [Kristus] bryter
        I Sarons vår.
Ljuvt i den röda kalken flyter
        En salig änglatår.

Med svaret flyger duvan åter
        Från ljusets fosterland
Till Anima, som tröstlös gråter
        I demiurgens band.
                    (*Bönen*, 1820?)

A beautiful flower there he [Jesus] breaks off
        In Saron's spring.
Delightfully the red corolla sheds
        A blissful angel tear.

With [this] answer flies the dove back
        From the fatherland of light

> To Anima, who inconsolably cries
> In Demiurge's chains.
> (*Prayer*, 1820?)

Though in the Platonic system "Demiurge" means a "deity who fashions the sensible world in the light of eternal ideas"—I have again quoted from my *Webster's*—in Stagnelius, who was, of course, a sort of Platonist, Demiurge is just a "bad guy."

Without a doubt, Stagnelius's mythology is far more sophisticated than what I have just attempted to describe: Its heroes are many, and each of them has a determined *emploi*. And I am not writing an introduction to Stagnelius. My goal is to show that everything that is personally metaphysical—like a poetic mythology, for example—grows up from a landscape with which a future poet has been presented from the very beginning. This landscape has the same metaphysical "inbornness" as his or her name. All heroes in Stagnelius are dressed in words/names from Greek or Latin, while they're walking Swedish shores indeed and with a "weather channel" kind of wisdom of how Swedish seas and skies behave.

11

Yes, the visual could apprehend the semantic. For those who haven't been to Sweden, I would recommend reconstructing Stagnelius's motionless—however very moody—metaphysical landscape from studying the black-and-white photos of my favorite, Ansel Adams, specifically his *Fiat Lux* series. Like, for example, his "Birds on a Beach, Evening," "Road to Leesburg," and "Fore-Pond Spill," which—all three—can be easily found in the California Museum of Photography. What of Stagnelius is in them? The same threatening hand from the Sistine Chapel ceiling, which is represented in them by a vast cloud hammering the idle water in "Fore-Pond Spill," or a water-like road in "to Leesburg"—in this photo it is the same hand but hanging down after the last attempt to reach the ground. The ground, that is, another hand: Adam's hand trying to touch God's. Am I paranoid? Adam's and Adams. . . . I don't think so. Moreover, I am almost sure that the great photographer had learned about his Adamic mission to give objects their names exactly from his own. And thus Adams started using his objective lens.

It happens that people match even in different times. Like thoughts, for example. This winter, after a long drive with my girlfriend, we pulled over in order to take a short walk down to Lake Michigan and see how it was behaving in the indifferent weather. The beach was, naturally, empty; there was no snow on it, but the sand looked like a deep-frozen dragon whose scales faced the water and recalled the toppled dunes. She stood closer to them than I, who was then thinking: "*This* is Stagnelius! Those are as morose as a wintertime Swedish shore." And exactly at that very instant when I was about to finish the first syllable of the last word from my tame thought about "Swe——," she—having never been there—suddenly asked, "Don't they look Swedish?"

It is no wonder to me that Adams looks like Stagnelius. Or, probably, it is Stagnelius who sounds the way Adams looks?

12

Well, from his Öland, Stagnelius moved to the twentieth-century "capital" of Tetra-Pak, Lund (1811), then to Upsala (1812), then to Stockholm (1816). There, he wrote and published (1817) his Homeric-Virgil-like epic *Wladimir den store* (*Vladimir the Great*), performed, naturally, in hexameters. In short—though it concerns a severely long narrative—it was all about Russia. As a Russian, I am, of course, pleased that Stagnelius was a Russophile: He—a distilled, so to speak, Protestant—also believed in the Russian Orthodox Church and in that "light" (remember? lost!) that should come from the East in order to rescue all stagnating humanity. Nowadays, we'd say that Stagnelius was a "mystical leftist": Russia was Christianized by his hero Vladimir for its own good but *forcibly;* Russia's ultimate "light," however, reeks with the bolshevism of 1917. Strange, but the Revolution, this fake projector of Russia, was switched on exactly a hundred years after Stagnelius's epic had been published. And still, how many European intellectuals— one hundred years later—have been just as dazzled by this "light"! Don't blame Stagnelius, though. He was a singer of "stagnation," and his voice was especially strong at night. Like a nightingale, worshiping his rose, he sang his night paeans bowing his head to the candle end.

13

"Natten är dagens mor, Kaos är granne med Gud"—"Night is mother of day, Chaos is neighbor with God," he wrote then. But in Stockholm, Stagnelius's life sank more and more into drugs and alcohol. His depression was constant. He couldn't sleep. One of his neighbors testified:

> Stagnelius would wake up the entire apartment building in the middle of the night with a hullabaloo, in a nightgown and with a poker in his hand averring that he just drove Demiurge out of his place.

It was already a delirium tremens.

He kept telling everybody that he would soon die. Stagnelius's friends and parents were almost sure that he was about to commit suicide: Some warm bath in cold Stockholm and his veins cut. Exactly like those Romans. But even while falling apart, he nevertheless continued with his writing and drinking, drinking and writing. While his "heart worm"—a romantic expression—was growing bigger and bigger, until it reached the size of an eel. He tried to slay it with more booze. But like the eel mother in the H. C. Andersen story, who only cried over her captured children after the fisherman washed them down with hard liquor, Stagnelius believed that his "worm" would only succumb to death by alcohol. Stagnelius was stagnating, and, tragically for him, his "heart worm" happened to be stronger than alcohol.

Indeed, all these "heart worms," when they become huge eels, inhabit one's soul entirely. And from then, the latter turns into an eel state, some, so to speak, Eelinois.

Noise of a heart, beating.

In 1823, Erik Johan Stagnelius died of heart failure.

14

Was it Archilochus (675?–635? B.C.) who wrote "I drink while leaning on my lance"? Yes, it was he, who was the first to employ the elegiac couplet, a future favorite of Horace, Ovid, and my Stagnelius. Because Archilochus was both poet and soldier, take this verse of his as both truth and metaphor.

Stagnelius's end: He drinks from a copper chalice while lean-
ing on an iron poker. He is nearly naked: His dirty nightgown
looks like some worn-out toga. He accomplished his most impor-
tant feat: He drove Demiurge out and set Anima free to return to
heaven. It's done. Stockholm is under the thin snow and deserted.

Stagnelius's childhood: He drinks a ray of sun while leaning on
it, whose tip made a hole in the cloud. Through it, he sees that the
blue exists. He is naked, like all boys, and wears only his name's
placenta. He is positive that he will be *us*eful. His beach is de-
serted, but the sand is still warm. (See sections 3 and 4.)

Two different deserts, and I'd choose the second, though I of-
ten find myself in the first.

Is it possible to stay in the second one forever?

I am not answering. For poets—and I shamelessly quote now
from my own section 3—are genetically acquitted deserters from
normal life.

I just love lonely beaches.

On one of those in Sweden there is a house, to which my Ameri-
can friend—while visiting me in the milk capital of Lund—brought
me. We—the hosts and he and I—drank leaning upon the last lance.
The view was a luminous black-and-white revelation slowly moving
toward a nighttime, with me trying to wrap it up into my visual car-
ton. And it's still there. "Because" I was then "from Lund," in which
people *know* how to wrap things up in order to prolong their exist-
ence. Stagnelius "wrapped" his life up into five black bricks, and
they made his pyramid—no, something even higher—in which he
lies at the age of twenty-nine. Still, everything—landscapes, moods,
liquids, cirri, cumulus, sounds, and memories—all of them demand
to be wrapped up, because they don't want to flow away.

> . . . You alone knew
> that motion is not different from stillness,
> that the void is the same as fullness,
> that the clearest sky is but
> the most diffused of clouds. . . .
> Yet it gives me no rest to know
> that alone or together
> we are one*

wrote Eugenio Montale in his *Xenia* (I, 14).

---

*I quote G. Singh's translation from *Eugenio Montale: New Poems*
(New York: New Directions, 1976).

And thus, everything which is just a sound in the beginning (like names) but is *realized* then into *destiny* (later) is already wrapped up. Everything that is put down is wrapped up.

15

Stagnelius's desert turned out to be too chilly. Imagine there a monument, a sort of Ozymandias:

> . . . Two vast and trunkless legs of stone
> Stand in the desert . . .
> Near them, on the sand,
> Half sunk, a shattered visage lies, whose frown,
> And wrinkled lip, and sneer of cold command. . . .

An obelisk broken down by drugs and spirits. Let us, however, recall Horace, such as he is performed by Ezra Pound:

> This monument will outlast metal and I made it
> More durable than the king's seat, higher than pyramids.
> Gnaw of the wind and rain?
>   Impotent
> The flaw of the years to break it, however many.

Lund, 1993, and 1245 Elm Street, Evanston, 1999

From the Book
Accidents, Coincidences, and Correspondences

The Poet of Flowers: Linnaeus

The revolutionary language so typical for the eighteenth century can be found in the annals of Swedish botany as well. Here is a quote from the founder of scientific botany, the Swede Carl von Linnaeus:

> The cemetery from which I take my soil can be considered a ground in which people are turned into people. For I take the soil to my cabbage patch and plant cabbage in it. Later, instead of a human head I take a head of cabbage from the garden, and I feed it to other people. So it turns out that we eat something that grew from human heads and other body parts. Thus, we eat our dead, and this is good for us.

Even on the basis of this fragment, you can tell that for this great Swede the world of plants was much more real, much more animated, than that of people. It could be said that this feeling is characteristic of Swedes to this day. In the course of Swedish history, thank God, many more heads of cabbage were cut off than human ones. But let's return to Linnaeus. The "king of flowers," as he was called in Europe, ascended his throne slowly but steadily. One can only marvel at the painstakingness of his work.

In his *Journey to Armenia* (in the chapter "In the Orbit of Naturalists"), Mandelstam wrote:

> As a child in little Upsala, Linnaeus could not have avoided visiting the fairs, could not have missed hearing the explanations proffered in wandering menageries. Like all children, he melted and swooned at the sight of a learned young man in boots with a whip, or in the presence of a doctor of fabulous zoology who praised a puma, waving his gigantic red fists around. . . .

There is one big mistake here, of course. Linnaeus did not grow up in Upsala, but in the Swedish provinces, and, therefore, the real explanation (we'll call it that) for his scientific interests is completely different.

Later on, Linnaeus was, in fact, in Upsala, but he was there as a poor student who had nothing to offer the world other than his intellectual riches. It was there that he met "the best flower in my garden," as he himself wrote, Sara Elizabeth Moraeus, the daughter of the famous Swedish scholar Johan Moraeus. It didn't take the girl's father long to figure out that his daughter's suitor was a young genius. And here, by the way, several lines of Swedish history come together. For Johan Moraeus was the nephew of Bishop Swedberg, the father of the great scientist and mystic Emanuel Swedenborg. At one time, Swedenborg's father had brought the young Johan Moraeus to Stockholm and had helped him to advance in a number of ways. And that is why Johan Moraeus was quite happy to patronize Linnaeus. Marriage, however, was an entirely different story. Moraeus set one condition for Linnaeus. He could marry his daughter only after he had become truly famous.

And Linnaeus began to work on botany, which had fascinated him when he was a child in the provinces. It became for him a kind of sublimation of sexual energy. Carl von Linnaeus's botanical celibacy lasted many years, and perhaps this explains why his description of the plant kingdom exudes such an elegant eroticism. The stalks of plants twine together and unwind, flowers open up their stamens and pistils. While reading this, I get the feeling that Linnaeus touched and caressed his flowers as if they were a woman's body.

Linnaeus traveled over half of Europe and all of Sweden describing plants and flowers in a large number of heavy tomes. One can say that he tried to catalog his passion, to "order" it in order not to be overwhelmed by it in the course of many years.

And it was only after the plant kingdom had been cataloged and described that Carl Linnaeus received Sara Moraeus as his bride.

To this day, Swedes respect Linnaeus more than their other great countrymen. This, despite the fact that his human qualities were not the finest, as one of his admirers told me. He was quite willing to climb over other people's backs, as it were. But he had a single goal—Sara Elizabeth. And people, as we saw in the fragment I quoted at the beginning of this essay, were no more important than plants, and plants lay at his feet with enviable humility.

In fact, Linnaeus discovered one of the main qualities of the Swedish character even in those days, when Swedish history was by no means as calm as it is today. We could even say that he touched the deepest strings of the Swedish soul. No wonder his books are and were read as if they were best sellers. This is how his admirer explained the Swedes' great love for Linnaeus, which is simultaneously an explanation of why the Swedes know more about botany than other nations. It is quite natural, he said, for even today (not even to speak about the eighteenth or nineteenth centuries), Sweden, especially in the North, is very underpopulated. Swedes lived more with nature than with people. Consequently, they understand nature better than they do human psychology.

It is not only the parks and gardens of Sweden that are decorated in the spring, but the monument to Carl von Linnaeus as well. Someone always puts a living flower in his bronze hand, and, to this day, he looks down at it with erotic curiosity.

Translated by Andrew Wachtel

The Poetry of Money

National symbols often end up on money. For example, the Swedish hundred-crown bill has plants and a portrait of the much-loved Carl von Linnaeus. And the fairly new twenty-crown note has flying

geese and a portrait of the Swedish writer Selma Lagerlöf. It's very
pretty money.

> Lapland—Lapland—Land of Laps
> I can see you from afar!
> Hail Land of Laps,
> The country of geese!

That's how Selma Lagerlöf's excellent fairy tale goes. And geese do,
indeed, fly to Lapland in the northern reaches of Sweden. But, re-
ally, one finds geese, ducks, and swans everywhere in Sweden and
not just in the suburbs but in the cities as well. At first, I was just
amazed. What bird is the most common in European cities? The pi-
geon, of course. But in Sweden, the most common birds are geese,
ducks, and swans. Lagerlöf's right. Every Swedish city or town has
a lake or pond where they live. In the Lund city park there is a huge
population of ducks: all sorts of species, each with its own distinct
plumage. Not to mention the ducklings, geese, and swans. Even
from my windows—flung wide open for summer—the only thing I
can see are these clamoring, naïve geese and ducks begging for
bread. At first, I wanted to leap from the window with my roasting
pan. . . .

So, anyway, one doesn't even have to fly to Lapland. Selma La-
gerlöf's fairy tale is great because you can derive from it an abso-
lutely faithful impression both of Sweden's flora and fauna and of
the particularities of Swedish life. Take, for example, the episode
where the villain, a fox named Smirre, is hunting geese and kills a
sparrow:

> When the animals saw that Smirre was trying to attack wild
> geese and that he had killed a sparrow, their rage was without
> limit. Even the vixens rose up against their own kind. Right on
> the spot they put him on trial. The verdict was read: He who
> breaks the eternal law of the world on the day of the great gath-
> ering of the beasts and birds, will henceforth be banished from
> the flock. Smirre the Fox has broken this law, and his paw will
> never again step on our land.

In this episode I think one can find the principles of Swedish democ-
racy—that is to say, equal rights and Sweden's famous neutrality.

Concerning sparrows. It is precisely the sparrow (the bird, I re-
mind you, that the fox killed) that Swedes often name as one of

their favorite birds. And this is not without reason. For the Swedes, the sparrow is the symbol of modesty, a quality not unappreciated in Scandinavia. The sparrow is often mentioned in Swedish poetry. For example, my favorite Swedish poet, Werner Aspenström, describes the sparrow this way:

> Sparrow—an exceptionally unexceptional bird.
> He hides in life, like ears of wheat in a field.
> His reddish plumage
> Is as plain as gray pavement.
> But his plans are colossal: he would live
> One day and then another
> Night and day.

True enough, it's not always successful in its plans. Even in a country as peaceful as Sweden, one finds evil foxes. Every Swede has his own favorite bird. But when I asked, not a single one of them nominated an exotic species. Even the principle soloist of the fauna world, the nightingale, wasn't named. Some chose the pheasant. Every once in a while I think that the pheasant for Sweden is like the cow for India. I remember driving once when a pheasant crossed the road. When it reached the middle, it stopped and turned its head. We couldn't go on until it had decided to move.

Without a thorough knowledge of birds, it's difficult to really understand Swedish poetry. Plants and birds are something of a genetic passion of the Swedes. For example, when reading the love lyrics of the Swedish poet Carl Wennberg, I stumbled across the tiercel. If not for an ornithological encyclopedia, I would hardly even have known that this animal has wings and that it was a bird. To my Russian ears, "tiercel" is a not terribly nice word—the words "peregrine" or "hawk" are much more comprehensible. It is precisely the tiercel, however, and no other bird, that flies over Swedish territory and turns the pages of Swedish poetry with its wings.

I'll give you another example. Owls. Lagerlöf, by the way, has a lot to say about owls. Unlike Russian, Swedish is a metonymic language. In my essay on the artist Hans Viksten, I compared some owls in his painting with Baudelaire's cats. I suddenly realized that the word for this species of owl in Swedish was *kattugla*, which literally means "cat-owl." In Russian, it is *neasyt'*—quite a fierce word but not at all expressive.

It's a splendid, hot summer in Sweden. I'm no longer amazed by the abundance of geese, ducks, and swans. Having once encountered the Swedish language, however, you begin always to expect the unexpected: be it the metamorphosis of a cat into an owl or the metamorphosis of flying geese into money.

Translated by Michael Denner

The Poetry of Trolls

The Swedes and other nationalities that inhabit Sweden are not alone: They share it with dwarves, gnomes, elves, and trolls. These other creatures settled in Scandinavia in days of yore. At first, they waged war against the Scandinavian pantheon, and later each in its own way impeded the spread of Christianity in Scandinavia. Even today, in modern research dedicated to Swedish history, one comes across allusions to the pranks of these creatures. For example, I read in one attempt to unravel the mystery of who shot Charles XII—the Norwegians or the Swedes—that only the trolls from the "Norwegian mountains" know this tragic secret.

Unlike the Scandinavian giants (which are called *jättar*), trolls always do harm to people. They are stupid, hideously ugly, and enormously strong. They live inside mountains, where they guard immense treasures. When Christianity was introduced to Scandinavia, the trolls tried any which way to prevent its spread. They threw enormous chunks of rock at churches under construction, and these stones lie scattered about Sweden to this day. They even call them *trollkast*, which means "troll castings." If you've never seen these huge stones, it's hard to believe that they really exist. These boulders always plagued the Swedish peasants, who were forced to cart them off their fields—an undertaking of no small scale. What's more, in their working of the land, the Swedish peasants upset the gnomes—creatures otherwise well disposed to humankind. Gnomes dislike field work, since it wrecks their underground kingdoms. Thus, the Swedish farmer is immediately beset by two malignant forces: the gnomes and the trolls.

But let's return to the time when the trolls were throwing their boulders. In principle, one could call these granite chunks the forerunners of Sweden's famous mysticism. Swedenborg, while he was still in his scientific phase, dedicated an entire paper to them. Trying to explain and clarify how the huge round openings that the Swedes call *jättergrytar* (giants' caverns) were formed and how the boulders came to be scattered about the country, Swedenborg—without recourse to trolls—came to the same conclusion as the ancient Swedes who so disliked trolls. According to Scandinavian mythology, the world arose out of the interaction of water and flame with the cold, and it will perish in fire and flood, cold and heat. And here is Swedenborg's explanation: At one time, the earth turned about the sun much more quickly than now, and therefore the days and years were significantly shorter. It was always springtime on earth, since there was hardly any difference between winter and summer. Paradise, in short. Anyone can verify this effect, says Swedenborg, by rotating a thermometer around a fire first quickly, then slowly. (By the way, the thermometer was invented by another Swede, Celsius.)

And this explains, claims Swedenborg, why the patriarchs of humanity lived so long and why, sometime in the future, the days will lengthen as the earth moves away from the sun. The earth will revolve more slowly, and the climate will become colder until the world completely freezes over. According to Swedenborg, the rocks came into being because of a fall in temperature caused by a worldwide deluge.

Another explanation of these mysterious rocks can be found in the myth about a certain dwarf who was courting the daughter of the god Thor. In order to prevent this marriage, Thor resorted to trickery, convincing the dwarf to remain outside until dawn, when the sun would turn him to stone. For those womanizing dwarves, who often kidnapped pretty women, could not survive any exposure to sunlight. Perhaps (using terms from Swedenborg's theory) there was a lot more light in somber Scandinavia in those days than there is now. In any case, this is another therein-lies-the-explanation for why so many laggard dwarves were left scattered about the country in the form of stones.

One more stab at an explanation. This one is entirely "domestic." In some verses by Werner Aspenström we find the following:

> Having read 73 chefs-d'oeuvre about Icarus alone,
> I want to render to Granite, his brother, what is owed,

So that on earth it remains standing for centuries.
I speak on behalf of the grasses and the beasts,
To whom he gave shade and protection against the rain.

Strange as it may seem, in their explanations of the source of the mysterious stones, both Swedenborg and Aspenström managed to avoid the gods of Scandinavian mythology. Unlike their Greek counterparts, Scandinavian gods are entirely mortal. Their absence in these explanations is yet another affirmation of this mortality.

A friend of mine, a Swedish woman whose husband runs a farm, stopped by her local library a while back to look up the names of the Scandinavian goddesses. She needed this information to find a fitting name for a newborn calf, whose mother was named Freya, after the head goddess of the Viking pantheon. In the library, they told her that the Vikings never had any goddesses, and, had it not been for my Soviet encyclopedia, a certain Swedish cow would have had to make do without a name.

And so it stands to reason that either the dwarves kidnapped all the women from Scandinavian mythology or that, to this day, trolls are out to get Swedish farmers.

Translated by Michael Denner

Solitaire of Coincidences: Balthus and Kevin

1

I would never have thought that figurative painting could still, to this day, disturb the viewer. But a year ago, in the Art Institute of Chicago, I was transfixed by a painting entitled *The Game of Patience*. Depicted in the painting is a sort of curtain or oilcloth in the upper left-hand corner, lifted slightly to open up a small gap. The hand performing this action is missing, however. But it really seems as though the hand is there, somehow, because the material so precisely imitates the effect of a hand. Thanks to this opening, we can see what is depicted in the picture. Or, at least, so it seems. This is, however, an illusion, since the curtain is in the left corner and the figure is in the center. But the center is here, on the left, and in the pseudo-center is a girl, about the age of Lolita. She is balanced on one knee on a green velvet ottoman and, parallel, on the same side, she's leaning on her elbow against a low rococo-style table. The other leg, in a dark stocking, is straight and the other arm embraces the edge of a table. Her head is exaggeratedly large, but the face is attentive and pretty. Her eyes are directed at the cards arrayed before her.

That's it—the entire picture. But such energy emanates from it, and there is such psychological depth displayed in this look through the metaphorical "gap," that it's difficult to tear oneself away. I found the name of the artist: Balthus. Born in 1908. "Strange," I thought, "I swear I have never heard of him before." I returned to Sweden from Chicago, and precisely a month later I was reading *Newsweek* and came across an article about Balthus entitled "The Last Great One" which contained some reproductions. One was of a girl—again, about the age of Lolita—sitting on a couch and holding a small mirror. She sits with one leg tucked under her, and her skirt has ridden up. Next to her other outstretched leg sits a cat. In the background is a lit fireplace.

A year later I was again in Chicago, and once more I went to the Art Institute to have a look at *Patience*, this time with an American friend. Seeing my raptures over the painting, he said, "They ought to put your Balthus into prison for perversion of minors!" And there's more than a measure of truth in his remark: Balthus's Lolitas, even when they're fully dressed, breathe such a mature, naked eroticism that, by comparison, any real nude hanging next to them seems to be bundled up in a fur coat.

From Chicago I flew to San Francisco, where, despite the heat, people go about dressed in fur coats. But enough about them. In San Francisco, I ended up in the studio of an artist named Kevin Kearney. The first thing I saw at the entrance was a large canvas entitled *Nostalgia for Lost Poverty*. The canvas depicts two chairs, a low table, a rug, and a small dog that looks more like a cat. I stopped in my tracks: I knew I had seen the chairs and rug somewhere before. But where? Of course, in Balthus's *Patience* and perhaps in his other painting, the one with the girl and the mirror.

Same for the cat (or dog). But where was the model? It was as if she had disappeared from the room.

"Maybe she's in the other room? And why the title *Nostalgia for Lost Poverty?*" I asked Kevin.

"You guessed it," he answered. "The model is really in the other room, and as for the poverty. . . ."

As we went into the next room (it was a large house), he told me his story. At about thirteen, Kevin realized that he was an artist of at least the same stature as, say, Ingres. He even met with early success. But at around thirty he was struck by a desire to do portraits of naked women. And so he painted a series of nudes, but for whatever reason no one bought them. He sold everything he had and bought a bunch of otherwise useless things that were essential to his paintings: old tables and broken-down chairs upon which he placed his models. Kevin showed me one of his paintings, and it made me gasp. Seated at a rococo-style table is a life-size naked woman peering into a mirror. Nothing is reflected in the oval mirror save the stark, unbearably blue California sky, the same sky seen through the oval window behind the woman's back. Both the figure and the face—my God, what beauty! The rug under the model's feet was the sole direct quotation from Balthus.

"Would you believe it?" said Kevin. "This is the only one of my nudes that I ever managed to sell."

"Why is it still here?"

"The buyer called me up about ten years later and asked me to take the painting back. Didn't even ask for money. Just said he couldn't live with it!"

Kevin showed me some of his other nudes. Balthus's Lolitas had grown up, and, as adults, one could get them to undress without being put in prison for perversion of minors. And, besides that, we were in California, where it's hot, and not in Switzerland, where Balthus lives and lights his fireplace.

But still, why *Nostalgia for Lost Poverty?* Having gone bankrupt on his nudes and finding himself living in a bare room furnished with two chairs, a table, and a Balthusian rug with a dog, Kevin gave up painting in despair and started a construction and design business. With that, he became rich. Having done so, he again began to paint, no longer dependent on the tastes of his buyers. But his nudes were put into the other room for good.

So what's the point of all this? It has nothing to do with the fact that beauty is dangerous. Enough has been said about that. I have in mind that fact that the whole world is rhymed. If one line—such as, for example, Balthus—shows up in Chicago, then its rhyme might very well show up somewhere like far-off San Francisco. Like Kevin Kearney. And why are rhymes drawn one to another? Probably because the poet is a magnet of coincidences. Or else because the kind of solitaire that artists play—the accidental sort— never ends.

2

A Cat, Arches, and Balthus
for F. Ingold

1

Your hand lifts the curtain and immediately
disappears, leaving behind a mini-arch,
big enough to contain your eye,
but look back—and

your pupil collapses . . . an avalanche. . . .
covered by eyelashes. Just like
when you jump from a hay stack
taking it with you

onto a parquet floor. . . . Logs crimson in the fireplace. . . .
A girl sits on an armchair, bending her
leg at the knee. And through that mini-arch
you see only ears

flattened against fur. . . . She stares
into a little mirror. You see
her pupils, eyelashes, and the blue-tinged fur
of a cat whose eyes blaze sparks.

2

A cat crackles like logs in a fire. Logs
in a fire crackle like a cat.
The reversibility of a metaphor is archlike. Two
crossed scimitars: which will win?

or a computer at an exhibition of Leonardo. . . .
The task: having taken the wind into account

raise the arch in such a way
that it does not collapse. . . . The answer:

Remember a string of pearls on your beloved's neck
with a big pearl at the top of her cleavage. . . .
It's the same with arches: the only ones that hold
are those with the heaviest stone in the center.

3
If I say "yes"—
stop me, because
I meant "no."

Sight—as always—
winds around the bend
and slides into a trench.

But we can forgive the pupil.
It sees the bend
above itself, the lining inside out,

a stocking over the knee. . . . That's how a cat frowns;
and a blue arch forms inside him,
making waves in his internal lining.

Translated by Michael Denner (essay)
and Andrew Wachtel (poem)

Gustav III

Somehow it happens that revolutions begin in "spaces for playing
ball." And not just French revolutions but Swedish ones as well. In
the latter case, to be sure, it's a "cultural" revolution that occurred
during the eighteenth century, in the reign of Gustav the Third.

My fellow Russians base what they know about the Swedish
monarchy on V. Pikul's novel, *The Favorite*. In the novel, Gustav
comes across as a severe master wearing the stiff boots of Charles
XII and, like Charles, dreaming of his own military success. He
was the aggressor, and the result was that he was crushed by the
army of Catherine the Great.

Don't believe the novel, gentlemen! It was not that way at all!
Believe me, instead! King Gustav was not a whit like this, and his
role was entirely different. It was a cultural role, and a tragic one.

But for now, let's return to our "space for playing ball," otherwise known as a tennis court. Even in the eighteenth century, the art of tennis was extremely well developed in Sweden (which is, perhaps, why Swedish tennis has had so many successes of late). But, you say, that's tennis. What about Swedish culture? It existed, of course, but the revolution arrived with Gustav the Third. It was Gustav who turned a tennis court, "a space for playing ball," into the very place where Strindberg and Bergman got their start: a theater. A real ace!

It was here, in this theater, that Sweden saw its first opera, *Thetis and Peleus*, in January of 1773. Remember this title, since it turns out to be quite symbolic. Why this opera was chosen and not another is simple: namely, *Thetis and Peleus* was set during the reign of Louis XIV, and Gustav III was a Francophile. The Swedish libretto of the opera was written by a certain Johan Wilander, one of Gustav's advisers (the funny thing is, one of the future stars of Swedish tennis was also Wilander). It began like this, more or less:

> We see here a field, alit by the rays of bashfully blushing
> Aurora, but, the Sun begins its ascent
> And the higher it goes, the louder, the more inspired
> The Genius must descant
> The age of Gustav!

(I'd like to draw your attention to the metaphor "blushing Aurora" as the color of the tennis court.) And so, set on a former tennis court, *Thetis and Peleus* heralded the Gustavian period of Swedish culture.

Gustav was an extraordinary fellow: poet, playwright, musician, and, of course, actor. He played the lead roles in eight of the twelve plays staged during a single season. True enough, it was in a different theater. Gustav began erecting theaters almost immediately. The biggest and most well known is the Opera, the very one built on the tennis court. Need I mention that Gustav was an architect as well? He did the blueprints for the building, which was the best operatic theater in Europe for its time. It even had central heating in the form of special pipes that emitted hot air built into the walls.

Theater and art were Gustav's passions. He was the first and last king-patron of the arts in Swedish history. The entire reign of

Gustav III was a masquerade, and even war was somehow nothing more than a change of costume.

Gustav was even patron for many artists beyond Sweden's boundaries, in particular for Beaumarché. When *The Marriage of Figaro* didn't make it past the French censors, Gustav (who read the work in manuscript) wrote to his "reigning cousin" Louis XVI to say that he found the play (and I quote), "more scenic than cynical" and was instrumental in the play's being staged in both France and Sweden. Sweden was the first country where *The Marriage of Figaro* was translated and staged.

Gustav III was an extraordinarily charming person, the lover of both men and women. The king was bisexual. And if Figaro's marriage was a success, his own was a failure from the day of its "premiere," when he was still a prince. It's even possible that it was through theater and writing that Gustav wished to sublimate the psychological and historical state he inherited from his mother, Queen Lovisa Ulrika. As a child, Gustav experienced what nowadays goes by the pleasant name of "the Oedipus complex," and to the end of his days his laughter (even at theatrical comedies, as his contemporaries noted) was always sad. . . .

Gustav III met an unhappy death, which brings us back to the beginning, that is, to the theater he directed. In March of 1792 (that is, "twenty years later . . . "), in the very same Opera, a costume ball took place, which the king, of course, took part in. During the event, a shot rang out: Gustav III was fatally wounded. He died the following day, the victim of a political enemy's bullet, at the age of forty-six, with the same sad smile that he wore even when happy (I know from the death mask). And thus ended the brilliant era of Sweden, the age of Gustav, about whom one Swedish historian wrote: "The sober realism of the king was accompanied by an exceptionally brilliant imagination which too often led him into the realm of fantasy." But those of us who aren't historians know what resulted from the marriage of Thetis and Peleus: Achilles. The theater turned out to be the "Achilles heel" of Gustav III. "In my beginning is my end," as Eliot put it.

Translated by Michael Denner

Twelve Stories about Swedenborg

The First

A citation is a cicada—Osip Mandelstam once said. Mysticism is sticky—I say. Which makes it hard to slide over the parquet floors of the eighteenth century.

I first heard the name from Alexander Revich. The owner of a unique piece dating from the eighteenth century, Revich would from time to time open that piece—a leather trunk—imperiously (it's not for nothing that his name rhymes with Tsarevich) in order to quote pearls and rubies in his rubylike voice. It was a strange name: Swedenborg.

At that time, many years ago, I neither connected Swedenborg's name with the country nor, even, with the name of the author of one of the epigraphs to *The Queen of Spades*. Do you remember? "That night the late Baroness von B—— appeared to me. She was dressed all in white and she said to me: 'Hello, Mr. Councilor!'" I suppose this happened because Pushkin wrote "Swedenborg" as "Schwedenborg." "Emanuel Swedenborg" was himself not written that way but as "Emanuel Swedberg" when he was born into the family of the Lutheran pastor Jesper Swedberg. When Jesper Swedberg became a bishop, his son promoted himself as well, changing his name from "Swedberg" to "Swedenborg," not without an eye to international fame. To be sure, at that time Emanuel's fame was not related to the reasons for which he would be cited by Alexander Pushkin and loved by Alexander Revich. At the time he changed his name from "Swedberg" to "Swedenborg," he was world famous as a scholar-scientist: anatomist, physicist, mathematician, geographer, and so on—something like Russia's Lomonosov. But a last name is a tricky thing, as is a first name. Both of them can have a peculiar effect on the artistic mind. "John Donne," for example, sounds exactly like his most famous poetic line (made even more famous by its use in Hemingway's title): "For whom the bell tolls? It tolls for thee!" Where did that line come from? Listen to the John "Ding-Dong" of his name. For whom does the English bell (ding-dong) toll? John Donne asks himself. And, quite logically, he answers: For you, old friend, for you! Or let's take another association for my Russian ear: Byron. Yes, "George," but also "Gordon." And "Lord." And, in Russian, "Gordon" and "Lord" together make "proud" (*gord*). Thus, to me, the sources of Byron's notorious romantic pride are hidden in his name. And this acoustic association does not hold just for me; it was true for the romantic generation of Pushkin, Zhukovsky, and Lermontov as well.

I, for instance, am constantly on edge whenever I hear French. The French are constantly saying *il y a,* and I keep thinking they are talking to me. I turn around, and no one is there—but the language has called me!

Language called Emanuel Swedenborg as well. He lived at the end of the seventeenth and the beginning of the eighteenth centuries. In other words, he lived in that period when Sweden was what would now be called a great power. And if, in Russia, "Lomonosov" now sounds like a boxer with his nose off (as a result of all of his battles, arguments, and so on), in his own day his name resounded in a different acoustic key because of its importance and its historical role. Recall the rhyme *Lomonosov—Slava rossov* (Lomonosov—Russia's trove). His name became a symbol of the nation, and his nose was left out, since Gogol had not yet been born. And one more acoustic association from the eighteenth century: Derzhavin, whose name was directly associated with the state. Derzhavin—*derzhava* (the latter means "state" in Russian). By Derzhavin's time, Russia was standing tall; it had become a power, and the leading poet of Catherine's reign became, quite naturally, the acoustic incarnation of the country. The same thing is true of Swedenborg. Having changed from "Swedberg," the Swedish equivalent of "Jones" or "Smith," to "Swedenborg," the future great mystic of all time also wanted to be the acoustic incarnation of his country and time. And the time of this onomastic switch was that of Charles XII. Naïve Americans, when they see Swedenborg's name for the first time, will always pronounce it "Sweedenborg," which is phonetically and linguistically (and in every other way) logical. Because "Swedenborg" is written with a *w* and not a *v*, and in Swedish *w* is used only for borrowed words. So in the most literal sense, Swedenborg became Sweden's castle (in Swedish, *borg* means "castle") for the entire world, first a fortress of science and then of mysticism. . . .

It remains a mystery why Pushkin wrote "Swedenborg" as "Schwedenborg." It is hard to imagine that Pushkin heard the name in one of the Swedish dialects in which *s* is pronounced like *sh*. Most likely, he got his "Swedenborg" from German, in which "Sweden" sounds like "Shvayden." The mysticism of names sometimes bleeds into the fate of their owners.

And sometimes it doesn't. What is France connected to in our consciousness? With many things, but probably not with Anatole France. And that is also a pseudonym. . . . But in the case of Emanuel Swedenborg, everything worked out perfectly.

In my case, it worked out like this. As it happened, for complicated personal reasons, I found myself living in Sweden. And soon after that, I moved to London for a while. My ears, as often occurs on an airplane, got a bit stuffed up. And having arrived in London, I understood that the name "Swedenborg" was buzzing in my ear and that it had been ever since the time of Revich, who taught me quite a bit. In London I was living in the BBC's dormitory on Prince's Square. And knowing that Swedenborg had lived in London, I was passively interested in where. . . . But I returned to Sweden without having found out.

There, I began to read everything in the libraries about Swedenborg; I don't myself know why. . . . And, in one of the academic biographies of Swedenborg, a real tome filled with everything, on the pages about his life in London I read the following: "In London Swedenborg lived at his cousin's house on Prince's Square." I practically fell off my chair. It turned out that we had lived in the same place! That incident seemed a great coincidence to me. . . . It's hard to avoid getting stuck on mysticism's stickiness!

The Second

It's hard to avoid getting stuck in mysticism's stickiness. . . . That is what happened to the great Swedish scientist Emanuel Swedenborg when he turned sixty-one. At the age of sixty, he removed the crucifixes from the wall, the final, Protestant, lock on the door that opened out onto the great unknown. According to his own admission, there was heard a voice from on high, and Swedenborg could not ignore it. And then he felt himself to be completely transparent: This world and the next communed within him (and through him), not recognizing any material barrier. He stripped off his clothes, took a walking stick with a heavy knob in one hand and a heavy pack in the other, forgetting to remove his wig. And just like that he walked through the streets of Stockholm, with his wig on his head. Powder from the wig covered his shoulders. . . . He looked like a miller who had awakened in the middle of the night. . . . But it was a clear morning. Swedenborg's path led to Stockholm's main church, and Hans Christian Andersen's story about the emperor's new clothes had not even been written yet. . . . As a result, everyone pointed at Swedenborg. Imagine the scene: A world-famous person, known by everyone, is walking stark naked down the streets of a major European city, his hometown, and he is walking as if he is wearing his best Sunday go-to-meeting clothes . . . naked but with a walking stick and a wig. The angels, who were later turned into clever tailors by Andersen, had already sewn the transparent clothes in which he felt as if he was in his Sunday best. . . . The unmasking holiday was happening: Swedenborg had gone to the main church in order to break with the official religion once and for all . . . to break with it and be quits. . . . On his way to the church, Swedenborg undid his stuffed pack and began to hand out money to the poor, who were standing by the entrance. Having done so, just as he was, stark naked, he fell face forward onto the pavement. . . . He had fainted, or, as he said later, he had fallen into a trance. His servants carried Swedenborg home, still in a trance.

This new type of exhibitionism caused an unheard-of scandal in Stockholm. It needs to be recalled that Swedenborg was not merely a famous scientist but also a nobleman, who regularly took his place in discussions in the Swedish Rikstag. In response to his actions, Swedenborg was dressed down in the palace by Her most threatening Swedish Majesty Lovisa Ulrika. Before her he stood, a respected old man (and in the eighteenth century, sixty was very old), and was not allowed to utter a word. Eventually, the queen finished lecturing him and asked what he had to say in his defense. Swedenborg answered, as Anna Akhmatova would many years later: "I heard a voice. . . ." Then he began to explain that the voice had ordered him to abandon forever all "scientific work" and become a "spiritual visionary." The queen shrugged, decided that the old man's brains had gone soft, and Swedenborg left.

Some time passed. Rumors were heard in the palace that the former courtier Swedenborg had abandoned this world and was now in contact only with the next. And that, thanks to his ties with that world, he was working as some kind of private detective in this one; like an early incarnation of Sherlock Holmes, he was solving the most amazing mysteries. In the palace, whispered rumors flew, while on the streets laughter accompanied recollections of the exhibitionism. Doctors proposed diagnoses, among which paranoia was the most popular. But rumors continued to sweep the court, and Lovisa decided to call Swedenborg in again. . . . The audience was set for the time the queen generally devoted to card playing. Lovisa Ulrika received Swedenborg sitting at a card table surrounded by courtiers. She asked Swedenborg a single question: What had been her brother's last words, spoken to her alone on his deathbed? Swedenborg promised to ask her dead brother that very evening and to return the next day with the answer. Having bowed, he left the room.

The next day at the same time, the card-playing hour, Swedenborg appeared before Her Majesty. "Well?" the queen asked. In the presence of all the courtiers, Swedenborg leaned over to the queen's ear and whispered a single phrase. Lovisa Ulrika shuddered and exhaled: "!" Silence reigned in the royal apartments, and

under the cover of this silence, Swedenborg left the palace—
forever. . . . What did he say to the queen, and what did the queen's
dying brother say to her? We have no idea. Both things were said
in a whisper. Mysticism is precisely a whisper that causes goose
bumps on your skin . . . like an ellipses on the page. . . .

The Third

Mysticism causes goose bumps to run over your skin, like ellipses
on a page, like the dots and dashes of Morse code, running like
goose bumps through the air. . . . In the eighteenth century Morse
code had not yet been invented, but goose bumps from the whis-
pers surrounding the mysticism of Emanuel Swedenborg ran
through Europe and reached the healthy body of Germany, forcing
Immanuel Kant himself to shiver.

It happened like this, I imagine. One morning, Immanuel Kant
walked up to the mirror and saw some kind of grammatical error
in his reflection. He did not like his double at all. "Eh, eh," said
Kant. And his name twisted itself in the mirror in accord with the
syllable he had just pronounced. The "I" became an *e*, and Imman-
uel Kant started to hate Emanuel Swedenborg.

But Kant was a thoroughly honest person, and to avoid being
charged with blind prejudice, he sent two letters from Königsberg
to the same London address. The first was meant for Kant's British
executor, one Sir Green, esquire. The second letter was inside the
first and was addressed to Swedenborg himself. In the first letter,
Kant asked Green to make haste from London to Göteborg, where
he would find Swedenborg, who had just returned to Sweden from
Europe. Kant requested that Green locate Swedenborg and give
him the second letter, in which Kant asked Swedenborg to be kind
to Green and, at the same time, if Emanuel Swedenborg had a free
moment, to explain in comprehensible German to him, Immanuel
Kant, the basic content of his mystical worldview.

In the first letter, to the Londoner, Kant also asked him to sniff
out as much as he could about Swedenborg himself, which, you
will agree, is clear evidence of an unhealthy interest.

With these letters in hand, Green set off (or more exactly,
sailed off) from London to Göteborg.

It was the month of July, and there were guests sitting at table in the home of one Göteborgian nobleman. It was a Saturday, and there were fourteen guests, one of whom was Swedenborg. They sat down at four o'clock in the afternoon. A dinner in the eighteenth century was a long process—between the appetizers and the main course there was time to write a short story. . . . But to make a long story short, toward six o'clock, just as they were about to set upon the real dinner, Swedenborg suddenly got up without saying a word and rushed out of the dining room. Exactly two minutes later, he came back in, finding everyone in a pose that would later be immortalized in the last scene of Gogol's *Inspector General*, and announced that a horrible fire had just broken out in Stockholm and that his own home might well burn down, because the fire had engulfed such and such streets in the Swedish capital. I'd just like you to recall that even with today's modern transport, to get from Stockholm to Göteborg takes at least six hours, so you can imagine how amazed and demoralized all the guests were at Swedenborg's news. Having told them this, Swedenborg left again and came back in approximately two hours. During this time, as you can guess, the guests had not been able to enjoy their food, but now Swedenborg announced that "thank God" (his own words), the horrible fire had been extinguished. It was about eight o'clock.

That same evening, rumors of the Stockholm fire spread like wildfire itself through Göteborg, and on the next morning, Sunday, Swedenborg was called in by the authorities to tell them what exactly had happened in Stockholm on Saturday. It was not until Monday evening (that is, two full days after Swedenborg's announcement) that a messenger arrived from Stockholm with news of the disaster. The next day, Tuesday, a courier brought details of the events, telling what had and had not burned in Stockholm, when the fire began, and when it was put out. All of these details agreed exactly with Swedenborg's story and with the time on the clock in the dining room when he ran out and in.

When Sir Green arrived in Göteborg, the entire city could speak of nothing else but the prophetic abilities of Emanuel, about which the Englishman later told Immanuel Kant. Swedenborg received Green himself. He promised that he would answer all of the questions posed by the German philosopher and that he would even include Kant's letter plus his answer in his next book about mysticism. The fastidious Green wrote to Kant that Swedenborg was by no means a charlatan but that he was, in fact, a prophet and "*ein opfenherzlicher* man" (that is, an open and pure-hearted individual). Nothing remained for Kant but to accept as fact that Swedenborg had prophetic abilities, but, despite this, he continued to take the Swede down a peg whenever the opportunity arose. Why?

This is my explanation. It is because the letter *i* in the name "Immanuel Kant" is, as it were, Kant himself. That letter *i* means "and" in Russian, and it always requires a comma before it in any complex sentence. Recall Kant's famous phrase: "The starry sky above me, and the categorical imperative in me." That *i* is the "and" that connects the heavens and morality. But the sound *eh* is nothing more than a placeholder, the ecstatic sigh of the crowd! The success of *eh* is irritating to *i*, just as practitioners of ESP on television irritate our morals. And it is completely irrelevant that *i* and *eh* don't mean the same thing in German as they do in Russian. The important thing is the conclusion. And the conclusion is simple: Mysticism is not merely something that contradicts so-called common sense; it is also something that evokes contrariness on all levels, even on the level of a mirror, in which left becomes right, and where Immanuel looks and sees Emanuel.

The Fourth

Mysticism alters a person, like a mirror which makes his right side his left and vice versa. It altered Swedenborg as well. And precisely, like a mirror. To be sure, it wasn't the kind of mirror we look into during the day, but rather the kind we look into at night. The mirror was the mirror of our dreams, what we now call our "unconscious." In the eighteenth century, no one had ever heard anything about any unconscious, but the first Freudian already existed. He was Emanuel Swedenborg. And it was just in this way, as a true predecessor, the very first one, that Jung read Swedenborg, by the way.

But we were speaking about mirrors. . . . Swedenborg understood his dreams as the reflection of that gigantic mystical world into which he tried to lead the rest of humankind. And, at the beginning, that world truly frightened him. In what way? Just as the

Gorgon's head frightened the entire ancient world until Perseus came along. Until Swedenborg's appearance, mysticism was a totally malevolent discipline, wrapped up in black poodles, like the smoke from burning witches. To look mysticism in the eye meant to get stuck in the Middle Ages. . . . But Swedenborg decided to look mysticism in the eye and to become a man of the future. And to do so, he reached into Perseus's bag of tricks. After all, if the other world is reflected so completely in our dreams, then a dream is a kind of mirror. All you have to do is to let the unknown world reflect itself, and as you reflect it back you can defeat it, just as Perseus did to the Gorgon. A dream is Perseus's mirrored shield, and if you look at the Gorgon in the mirror, you don't have to worry about your eyes.

In Mandelstam you will find the lines: "Pour dreams, like blood samples, from one vessel to another." That is about Swedenborg the dream seer. Seer-prophet. . . .

So Swedenborg set to work. But when they are exposed to light, dreams are like dust bunnies in a draft. And that is why Swedenborg became the first person to begin writing down his dreams, enumerating them logically, and, having written them down, analyzing them. That is how an entire book came into existence: a thick ledger of such analyses entitled *Journal of Dreams.* . . .

Number 171 was the decisive mirror for Swedenborg. In it, he saw the reflection of his mystical wife. Here is the dream, translated from the Latin.

> Afterward, through an entire night, something holy was dictating to me, and the dictation ended with the words "sanctuary." I discovered that I was lying in bed with a woman and I said: "If you are not the one who said 'sanctuary' then we will complete the act." I turned away from her. With her hand she touched my member and it began to grow, becoming bigger than it had ever been. I turned toward her and bent down, and it tautened going in. She said that it was large. During the act I thought that it would produce a child, and everything worked out beautifully. This all took place alongside another bed from which a different woman was spying on us, but she went away before we made love.

Freud would have rubbed his hands with delight had such a dreamer appeared before him, but Swedenborg was his own Freud.

The dream is a testament to our utmost love of the holy, for all love comes thence. And it is cyclical, and the love in our bodies is bounded and is reflected in semen; when I entered her completely and found myself inside of her, it was completely innocent, which indicates that my love was a love of wisdom. The first woman was the incarnation of truth, and the second, who listened and in whose presence nothing happened, means that one should not speak about the truth and that no one should know of it. For to pronounce it is to defile what was originally pure.

Thus it was that Swedenborg came to know the truth, and from that dream forward all of his sexual needs were satisfied only in sleep and only with that woman. The high point of their relationship came in dream number 397. Here it is. "Just after dinner," Swedenborg writes,

> when I was asleep, a woman appeared before me. I did not see her face, but she was plump and all dressed in white. I wanted to invite her to have a drink, but she said there was nothing, but someone who was standing behind her back gave me permission to take the glass she was hiding in her clothing. While she was searching for the glass I saw that she was plump, as if pregnant. Having searched in the sleeves of her garment she drew out a glass, and although it was filled with hot chocolate, it was wine. I did not want any chocolate and I awakened immediately. It seemed to me that once or twice after awakening I perceived the smell of wine. I was especially intrigued by the white dress. I can't say for sure whether it was a woman, but the word "holy" was definitely spoken. I did not see her face but she was pregnant, which might mean that I am now on the proper path. For from that day forward I felt myself completely aware of the truth that I intend to make known.

A bit later, Swedenborg comes to the conclusion that because she was pregnant this was the same woman he had come to know some two hundred dreams before; that her white garments were a sign of her innocence despite her pregnancy; that the desire to drink wine meant a desire for intimacy with God and that the lack of desire to drink hot chocolate signified a refusal of earthly blandishments; and, finally, that the fact that the chocolate was simultaneously wine, and especially the fact that he could smell it upon awakening, indicated that he had been offered communion and had accepted it.

For the rest of his life, Swedenborg continued to have a relationship with this woman alone. He called her his wife. She bore him a child. Swedenborg had no sexual relations with any earthly women, but in his mystical mirror he sinned all the time. Holding his dream mirror shield, Swedenborg behaved like Horace in Pushkin's adaptation; that is, he threw it down and ran from the battlefield of dreams into the Epicurean life of a mystic. Horace, a great connoisseur of sexual delights, had the walls and ceiling of his bedroom covered in mirrors so that he could watch himself during sex. Swedenborg went much further than this: He fathered a child with a mirror.

Mysticism is a mirror. For what is the Trinity if not a tailor's tripartite mirror, in which one is reflected as three? A tailor's mirror is a mirror with wings. An angel, Swedenborg would have said.

The Fifth

A tailor's mirror is a mirror with wings, like an angel. In the eighteenth century, everyone went crazy for garden architecture, and Swedenborg employed the tailor's mirror as an innovative design feature. Swedenborg's garden in Stockholm was luxurious, particularly the flower beds, which began just beyond a gazebo in the garden's central alley. In the gazebo, Swedenborg set up a gigantic three-sided mirror at a special angle. When visitors entered the gazebo they stopped dead with amazement—before their eyes were three separate gardens, and a smiling Swedenborg asked them to choose which one they would like to walk in. . . . In the tripartite mirror of my story there are also three stories, and the first one is comical.

A little girl by the name of Greta lived next door to Swedenborg, and she frequently ran into his garden, where she was allowed to play. When Swedenborg himself appeared in the garden, she began to pester him, asking to see the angel. "Uncle Swedenborg, show me the angel," Greta importuned, and one day he gave in. He brought her into the gazebo and led her up to the tailor's mirror, now covered with a cloth. "Now you will see an angel," said Swedenborg, and he pulled away the cloth. And thus Greta saw an angel. . . .

The angel continued to fly around Swedenborg's garden, and various people came frequently to converse with the owner there. One of those regular visitors was the Russian ambassador in Stockholm, Count Osterman. One day, he was accompanied by an acquaintance, the widow of the former Dutch ambassador to Sweden. The widow was practically hysterical: She had unexpectedly received a bill for twenty-five thousand guilders (an enormous sum at the time), but she was sure—knowing her late husband's punctiliousness in pecuniary matters—that it had been paid before his death. She had dug through all his papers, however, and could not find any receipt acknowledging payment. Swedenborg promised to try and meet up with her husband in the other world and to find out what the story was. In a couple of days, Swedenborg asked Count Osterman to tell the widow that her husband would himself appear before her with an answer and to say that he could tell her nothing more concrete. A few days later the late husband did indeed appear to his widow and, in her own words, said: "Don't worry about the receipt, my child! Pull my desk drawer out all the way. It got stuck between the back of the drawer and the desk." This vision appeared at two o'clock in the morning, and the widow immediately jumped out of bed, called her maidservant, and headed for her husband's study. Having pulled out the drawer, just as she had been directed, she found not only the receipt but also a ruby brooch which she thought she had lost a long time ago. The widow went back to sleep happy, but early in the morning Swedenborg came to visit and woke her up. The confused widow had not even had time to tell him about what she had discovered when Swedenborg, in an unusually agitated state, told her that the previous night he had met her late husband who did not wish to speak because he was rushing to see his widow in order to tell her something important. It was only after that that the widow, now fully awake, told Swedenborg what had happened. . . .

The third story of our triptych is connected with Russian history. We know about it from notes taken by a Swedish nobleman who was quite skeptical regarding Swedenborg. It took place during a society party during which the nobleman happened to be standing next to Swedenborg, who was conversing amicably with a whole group of people. Suddenly, in the midst of the conversation, Swedenborg went pale and almost fell. He recovered quickly, but his swoon was noted by many observers. Having come to, Swedenborg began to speak very quickly, and he demanded that the time and date be noted. When the date had been written down—July 17, 1762—Swedenborg announced that the former Russian emperor Peter III, who had recently been deposed by his wife, Catherine, had been strangled in the prison to which he had been confined. The date turned out to be exactly correct.

So it is that our image in the mirror standing at the end of the alley comes fully, albeit gradually, into focus. We walk down the alley, and we see something at the very end. And only as we approach the end and the mirror do we perceive that we are seeing ourselves, whom we did not recognize at the beginning of our walk. Like the angel that Greta saw in her own person. Like the receipt found by the widow's own husband. Like the Russian emperor Peter III strangled by his own wife. A tailor's mirror is nothing more than your own face, seen from three sides at once. Even if the mirror stands in the garden of a foreign (and quite mysterious) mystic.

The Sixth

In Swedenborg's Swedish garden, at the very entrance stood an enormous mirror. It stood there long before any mirror ran into the garden of Russian poetry: "Along a path into a garden, in chaos and disorder, a looking glass runs toward the swings." The Swedish garden was well taken care of, like all parks and gardens in the eighteenth century—no chaos here. But at night, the mirror grew dark together with the rest of the garden, and Swedenborg's glance flew up to the biggest, exclusively nocturnal mirror: the moon.

We know from Ariosto that on the moon one can find vials, bottles, and tubes containing human reason. We know that the flag of the United States flutters there. It would be interesting to know which tube got smashed by the American astronaut who stuck his flag into the lunar soil. In any case, after this event, some terrestrial Orlando suddenly became sane, was let out of the asylum, and joined up with the rest of the New York homeless.

In between Ariosto and the astronauts, however, the moon was visited by Emanuel Swedenborg, who was considered no less insane than Orlando. To be sure, he did not go there to recover his lost—according to the doctors and other intelligent people—sanity, since Swedenborg did not consider himself crazy. The mirror in his Swedish garden reflected absolute order, and his lunar mirror reflected exactly the same order. It was the order that governed the mirror of his mystical theories, and the natural disorder that, according to Lewis Carroll, governs the world through the looking glass.

Nevertheless, all of Swedenborg's reflections (which he called correspondences) were secondary, so to speak, because the primary reflection, according to Swedenborg, belongs to God. The reflection of God's thought is the so-called Great Being, the infinite cosmic body that contains spirits and souls. After death, we enter into that Great Being, and we remain there until such time as we find our unique place.

The astronaut Swedenborg landed on the moon protected by the helmet of his powerful theory. In his hand he held a white flag of the type usually employed to begin negotiations. He awaited the spirits, and they appeared with alacrity. Swedenborg's account can certainly be considered absurd or comical, but it must be considered serious. According to Swedenborg, those spirits (or our former and eternal souls) who live on the moon (or who are forced to do so for some time) spoke to him in a strange manner. Because the moon has no atmosphere, the local denizens cannot use their lungs to produce the vibrations necessary for normal speech. As a result they did not speak with their stomach muscles (this version, which he calls *diaphragmation,* Swedenborg mockingly rejects), but with that part of the esophagus that normally produces burps. The lunar spirits burp their speech.

For those attuned to Russian phonetics, this might seem impossible, but it does not seem strange to a Scandinavian. In Danish, for example, there are a series of so-called guttural sounds which are quite reminiscent of those that Swedenborg speaks about.

For *Star Trek* fans, I can only say that the astronaut Swedenborg's interplanetary travels far surpass anything that happens on that show. Among other planets, I'd just like to mention Jupiter.

According to Swedenborg, the spirits that inhabit Jupiter rather than the moon are able to express themselves directly in the language of mirrors. That is to say, their faces reflect what they want to say. To put it another way, their language is the language of mime. Swedenborg, who was a scientist in addition to being an astronaut, explains that the basis of all languages is mime. According to Swedenborg, the word as such exists only on the earth. The Word was given to humans in order to allow them to understand their Creator, and our World is, so to speak, the center of the Word, because it was precisely on our World that the Creator allowed himself to be born again. According to Swedenborg, even Adam at first was capable only of mimicry; only later did he receive the gift of speech.

Thus, to put it very roughly, the spirits who inhabit Jupiter take up the space in the Great Being that is occupied in our brains by the power of imagination.

Swedenborg not only accepted the idea of multiple worlds (an idea by no means orthodox in the eighteenth century), he calculated them. Or, to be more exact, he counted them up in the course of his visits. He lists a million of them. Their two hundred generations of inhabitants add up to some three hundred million spirits.

In his eighteenth-century days, Swedenborg visited a lot of planets, but he began precisely with the moon. Humans in the twentieth century are repeating his pattern. And just between us, I am inclined to take Swedenborg's planetary theories very seriously.

A story says that one of the American astronauts who stepped onto the moon with a flag in one hand and with a camera—that most perfect version of a mirror—in the other succeeded in planting the flag but dropped the camera . . . from fright, it is said: He saw something on the moon that caused him to find religion after returning to the earth, where he became a quiet minister. It is quite possible that he was frightened by the Danish phonetics of the lunar spirits who merely tried to talk to him as they had earlier with Swedenborg.

The Seventh

When Robinson Crusoe found himself completely alone on an uninhabited island, he attempted to fill the emptiness with a large quantity of prosaic and useful tasks. In other words, he tried to create a normal existence and began to make furniture, graze goats, grow grain, and so on. Defoe published his novel in the sixth decade of the eighteenth century, and at the end of the seventh, also in London, Swedenborg's final work, *True Christian Religion*, appeared.

By no means am I attempting to find parallels between *Robinson Crusoe* and *True Christian Religion*. But after having lived in Sweden for five years, I found it necessary to reread Defoe. Because Sweden has a phenomenal ability to make people feel lonely. People in Sweden are so distant from one another that to live like latter-day Robinson Crusoes is their only salvation. Swedes are practical, like Defoe's hero, and their lives are full of hundreds of little tasks—they work in the garden, grow flowers, fix up their houses, and so on. They rarely interact with one another. But what can a person do if he is unable to fill his life with these occupations? The solution is simple: He can create interlocutors, immersing himself in a world of voices, as if it were a radio. What is more, the voices are real. And where there are voices, there are also visions; that is, televisions. Having united within himself the radio and the television, Swedenborg was a lone figure in the eighteenth century, like a radio tower on an uninhabited island. After all, Protestantism implies empty churches—not an image in sight.

The visions of the Protestant Swedenborg were, in fact, nothing more than the creation of forbidden icons and their transfer from visual to literary language. His description of the other world glows with Catholic gilt, and the strongest impression they produce is of Catholicism. Take Swedenborg's description of his meeting with the Mother of God, for example:

> Here is a fact I cannot ignore. Mary, the mother of Jesus, once floated above my head, all dressed in white. For one moment she stopped and said that she was only the mother of Jesus when she gave birth to him. But, having become God, he cast aside all the human essence that he had received from her. Now she herself considers him to be her God. She does not wish us to speak about Jesus as her son, because in Him there is nothing but godliness.

The relationship between reality and imitation, however, between life in this world and in the other world, is what concerned the spiritual voyager Swedenborg most of all. This is because, according to Swedenborg, we live in a world that is merely a simulacrum of the real one. And in that real world, people live according to the degree of their own imitation, religious in particular.

This is how Swedenborg describes the existence of a Moslem in the other world, for example. "In the other world Moslems live in the West, on the border of the territories of the papists. The reason for their physical closeness to the Christians is simple—Moslems accept our God as the Son of God and as the greatest of prophets who have come to earth to set people on the path of truth. It must be noted," continues Swedenborg,

> that all the inhabitants of the other world live at the exact physical distance from the Godhead as their religions are from true belief in God. The Godhead itself is to be found in the East. The enmity between Christians and Moslems stems first of all from their refusal to accept the Holy Trinity, which they perceive as a type of pantheism. They dislike the Catholics in particular, because the Catholics genuflect before images. They call them idol worshipers. Moslems insist that the Catholic God has three heads, that they speak of one God, but bow down to three of them.

As we can see, according to Swedenborg, the true religion is divided up in the religions of our world just as light is divided by a prism.

Having spent some time in Amsterdam, where he walked by the windows of the jewelry stores, Swedenborg saw how the light played in the precious stones, and his eyes blazed, not from greed but from the aptness of the analogy. "In the other world," writes Swedenborg,

> Jews generally go in for trade, just as they do in this one. They keep various stores and businesses where they sell precious stones which they get in the heavens (where there are quite a lot of such stones) in a manner unavailable to anyone else. The reason that they in particular get these precious stones is because they read the Word in the original, in a language in which each letter has holy significance. Each precious stone is equivalent to one letter of that language, and represents one letter of the Word itself. The Jews know how to work any stone in such a way as to make it look genuine. But for this they are cruelly punished by their heavenly leaders.

Genuine stones, fake stones. "Genuine Christianity" can also be easily faked, but Swedenborg does not say who punishes false religious carats and how.

He died a year after the publication of *True Christian Religion*, at the age of eighty-three, and he lies, like a lonely island, in the cathedral in Upsala, in a marble (real, I might add) tomb.

The Eighth

I collect angels. I have two favorites. One of them is plasmodial; it came out of some cellular-amebic state, and it flies around in the night sky, like any self-respecting angel should. The other, which has paper wings made out of Swedish newspapers, was created by Igor Ganikovsky long before I moved to Sweden.

In those long-ago days, Igor Ganikovsky had no idea that I would have a Swedish future, nor did he know that in the world of mysticism angels fly on the Swedish wings Emanuel Swedenborg made for them. But what are angels, really? According to Swedenborg, children who die become angels, and it is only in this case that mystical laws allow for an exception. Because, after their death, children continue to grow until they reach a certain age, but everyone else in the other world remains exactly the same age they lived to in this world. For children, there exists a kind of angelic nurturing, or an angelic boarding school.

Swedenborg writes:

> As soon as a little child is resurrected, which happens immediately after death, it goes to heaven, where it is presented to an angel who, in her mortal life as a woman, loved children and the Creator. This happens because although children are not angels, they become angels. Children are born into evil like everyone else, but like angels they must be kept from evil and given over to the good that is hidden inside them. That is why children need to grow up in heaven, for they need to grow up in order to come to know their own nature and make a correct choice.

According to Swedenborg, there are only two things that turn a potential angel into a real one. These two things are intelligence and wisdom. Since children have neither, they are not yet angels, although they stay with the angels all the time after their death. The angels are their scout leaders, as it were. But, as soon as they have imbibed the angels' lessons, as soon as they have acquired intelligence and wisdom, the children stop maturing and become angels themselves. Swedenborg concludes: "It needs to be proved that in heaven children grow until about the age of sixteen and then stay at that age forever."

As far as other attributes of angelhood go, Swedenborg lists quite a few. Angels, for example, have no sense of time. Swedenborg writes that the more angelic an angel is, the less he thinks about the past or concerns himself with the future. Their angelic happiness consists precisely of this, for only God tells angels what to think and how to behave at any given moment.

To continue: Angels, according to Swedenborg, possess complete freedom, despite the fact of their total dependence and direct subservience to the Creator himself. Thus, angels of the third rank—that is, the wisest of the angels—incarnate freedom itself.

Angels are always naked. According to Swedenborg, nakedness corresponds exactly to innocence. Nevertheless, despite the absence of clothes and the fact that they are unarmed, any angel is stronger than ten thousand men in this world because an angel's strength is not his own, writes Swedenborg, but from God. If for some reason an angel suddenly dares to think that his strength comes from himself, he immediately becomes weak and loses the ability to fight off evil spirits.

Angels are rather talkative and extremely frank, and Swedenborg was acquainted with quite a few of them. Still, you wouldn't call them chatterboxes. The reason for this paradox is that one angelic word is worth something like one thousand words pronounced by humans. As their Swedish interlocutor wrote: "Any word of angel language contains an infinite number of things for which our languages either have no words or for which there are too many meanings."

The two angels flying in my house correspond in one way or another to Swedenborg's description. The plasmodial angel is like a child who is becoming an angel through a long process of angelic natural selection. The angel who flutters wings of Swedish newspapers is like the many words in a single word heard by the ear of my fate.

After Swedenborg died and found himself amidst the angels, he was able to prove the correctness of his theory. Despite the fact that popular mythology loves to surround heroes with children (recall any politician kissing babies), the picture of Swedenborg surrounded by angel youths hangs high and amazingly beautiful.

The Ninth

On the sixteenth of June 1762, the Swedish nobleman Prince Klas Ekeblad went for a walk in one of Stockholm's parks. This spot is still called "the king's garden," although the park and garden disappeared long ago. But they still existed in the eighteenth century, and the Swedish nobility loved to promenade there in the hopes of meeting their king. Having come back home, Ekeblad wrote down the following in his—still preserved—diary. I quote:

> How pleasant it is to observe human predictability! When you see one or another man, you can always guess precisely what kind of woman will appear at his side. There was a big crowd in the king's garden today, and His Majesty was constantly stopping, the better to allow his loyal subjects to get a good view of him. Their curiosity is at times hilarious. Swedenborg was there, too, and he told me . . .

I break off the quotation here to say something about the genealogy of Klas Ekeblad, for it explains his somewhat haughty tone. On his mother's side he was a Gardie, and his grandfather, Magnus de la Gardie, had been the favorite of Queen Christina, which allowed his heirs to consider themselves directly connected to the royal family. Magnus de la Gardie had died comparatively young, in 1741, some twenty-one years before the events described here. And now we can continue the quotation. So, "Swedenborg was there, too, and he told me that my grandfather Magnus had recently married the Russian empress in heaven, a fact I consider it necessary to record because of its immense interest." Which Russian empress did Swedenborg have in mind? We can find the answer to this question in another diary, a "spiritual" one that was penned by Emanuel Swedenborg himself. There, Swedenborg provides an inspired description of the meeting between Magnus de la Gardie and Empress Elizabeth, who had died in January 1762, at the age of fifty-three, and who had ascended the Russian throne in 1741, the very year in which Magnus had died. According to Swedenborg, in the other world Magnus de la Gardie had

been separated from his first wife because of their "intellectual in-
compatibility." As for Elizabeth, she had immediately been sur-
rounded by crowds of suitors, but she showed no preference for
any of them, finding them all, "unharmonic," as Swedenborg puts
it. In the end, however, Magnus, who had been pining without a
wife for twenty-one years, met Elizabeth, and they knew that they
were meant for each other immediately. Swedenborg was also
aware of the reason for their compatibility. "For Elizabeth had
ruled the Russians, and Magnus de la Gardie had ruled over a large
quantity of souls while waiting for her, and both of them had ruled
in exemplary fashion." When Magnus and Elizabeth decided to
marry, here is what happened next in Swedenborg's description.
An angel all dressed in beautiful white clothes was dispatched to
sanctify the marriage ceremony. Having asked whether their de-
sire to be joined in marriage was mutual, the angel strengthened
their union with God's blessing. This solemn event took place, ac-
cording to Swedenborg, on March 5, 1762, three months before
the meeting of Klas Ekeblad and the Swedish mystic in the king's
garden.

Swedenborg's detailed concern with the posthumous fate of
the Russian empress does not end here, however. Another incident
relating to it was recorded by a friend of Swedenborg's named Carl
Robsahm. One day Swedenborg invited this friend to meet a Rus-
sian priest by the name of Oronoskov, who was attached to the
Russian diplomatic mission in Stockholm. Oronoskov was a great
admirer of Swedenborg, and he asked him to recount whether he
knew what was happening in the other world to Elizabeth (whom
he also admired). According to Carl Robsahm, Swedenborg re-
plied: "I see her frequently, and she is extremely happy." Seeing
tears in Oronoskov's eyes, Swedenborg continued: "Elizabeth's
good deeds in this world were properly valued in the other, for it
turns out that Elizabeth never did anything without first praying
to the Creator and asking for His advice and support to rule her
country better."

Swedenborg returned to the posthumous fate of Elizabeth one
other time. This took place at a dinner at the house of the Swedish
consul in Copenhagen. When asked whether he knew anything
about the posthumous fate of the Danish king Frederik V, Sweden-
borg said that he did and that the dead king was completely happy.

This was true of pretty much all the members of the Oldenburg family, he added, but the same could not be said about the Swedish kings. Swedenborg added, however, that no ruler in the other world has been honored as much as the Russian empress Elizabeth, because she had a good heart despite the many mistakes she made. . . . According to Swedenborg: "She had to sign a large number of documents that she did not have time to read because of their quantity, but every time, having returned to her rooms, she bowed down in prayer and asked the Lord to forgive her if she had unwittingly signed something she should not have."

But why do I write about all of this? To give Russians a chance to be happy with their rulers for once. Still, it is sort of a shame that in the heavens Elizabeth had to marry a Swede, and not our Russian Lomonosov or her terrestrial favorite, Shuvalov. Still, we can recall Lomonosov's lines dedicated to Shuvalov: "Oh, Shuvalov, those in our world / are wrong who think glass worse than minerals."

And let's not forget that in the old days Stockholm was called Glass City by Russians. Perhaps, then, we will understand why Elizabeth, as if heeding Lomonosov's advice, preferred a native of the glass city in the other world. Rulers should listen to poets!

The Tenth

Emanuel Swedenborg had great admiration for Charles XII. They became acquainted in Lund, where the court was located before Charles's final, Norwegian, campaign. Swedenborg was around thirty at the time. He was already famous as a mathematician and engineer, but he was not yet a mystic. Charles XII was no miser, but Sweden had been ruined by years of war, and even the king's court was in straitened circumstances. They ate off tin plates, for example. This led Swedenborg to write a tract entitled "How to Keep Tin Plates from Tarnishing," in which he went over in detail everything necessary to keep tin plates shiny.

Charles was readying his Norwegian campaign and employing the engineering talents of Swedenborg, who, for his part, attempted to interest the king in astronomy. Nothing came of the astronomy, but the campaign began.

The army consisted of sixty thousand well-equipped soldiers who, it must be said, loved Charles. And although the Danish blockaded all outlets to the sea, thereby rendering the powerful Swedish navy helpless, Charles decided to repeat the glorious feat of Hannibal. Having waited until the winter freeze, he led his army across the ice and over the high Norwegian mountains in order to attack the Danish rear. Now the Danish fleet was helpless, and, without a murmur, the Norwegians began to surrender to the Swedes, who became the masters of Norway in a few days. Only one Norwegian fortress would not surrender. It could not be stormed, so Charles settled down for a long siege. To ferry provisions and ammunition to the besiegers was no problem: Small ships managed to evade the Danish warships. It was only when Charles decided that he needed his navy for the successful prosecution of the siege that there occurred the great epic moment in which Swedenborg was to play a crucial role.

The ancient Greek argonauts, we recall, carried their boat on their shoulders over a waterless desert. Swedenborg thought up a device that would allow ships to be carried over mountains, much like the one that plays a starring role in Werner Herzog's film *Fitzcarraldo*. There, the action takes place in South America at the beginning of the twentieth century, of course, but the principle is the same—winches and tree trunks. According to Swedenborg's plan, the latter were placed under the ships' keels, and the ships were dragged with winches and ropes. In the course of seven weeks, some one thousand men managed to pull the greater part of the Swedish fleet over the mountains. When the ships were launched, they immediately gave battle to the large Danish fleet, which they defeated. Description of this event is preserved in the Swedish eighteenth-century chronicle. Here it is:

> Over wild mountains overgrown with pines moves a procession never before seen. Gigantic, clumsy ships are being dragged by hundreds of sailors and soldiers. We see here the elegant figure of the king himself surrounded by his generals and soldiers in their blue uniforms with gold piping, in their three-cornered hats and high boots. In this colorful crowd one can make out a young man in civilian dress, but with the fire of genius in his glance. That is Emanuel Swedenborg, who made this incredible feat a reality.

Of course, the Swedes would have taken the fortress, but Charles fell during the siege and great Sweden fell apart like Greece after the death of Alexander.

Swedenborg cried bitterly for his hero, and many years later, having become a mystic, he began to meet regularly with Charles in the other world.

Swedenborg did not like to share the impressions that those visits made on him, for they were too emotional. Because he continued to deify Charles, even in his mystical old age. And this, according to Swedenborg himself, was the whole problem. This love (we read in Swedenborg's letters) almost destroyed his immortal soul, because those who strive for domination in this life become extremely destructive in that one. According to Swedenborg, even though Charles XII had been very pious and wise in this life, in that life his passion for domination had become impossibly strong and threatened to eclipse all his terrestrial accomplishments. Swedenborg himself was barely able to get away from Charles's pressure in the other world, and did so only by making Charles so angry that the two broke off all relations. In the other world, and I quote,

> It turned out that in his boundless love of glory the king has lost all concern for his country. He was the most stubborn of mortals, and, having held a conviction, he had never once given it up. His pride was so gigantic that in the confines of this world it could never be preserved. Therefore, in the other world, Charles is surrounded by souls of some other, not earthly, origin.

"But the funniest thing," writes Swedenborg, "is that in the other world Charles XII has gotten married to a woman very much like himself and who is even more stubborn. As a result, he has to submit to her."

So, with the help of Swedenborg, in this world Charles XII was able to do what Sisyphus has still never been able to do in the other: He pushed not a rock but an entire fleet of ships to the top of a mountain. But in the other world his fate is no more enviable than Sisyphus's: Having ground the Norwegian mountains under the heel of his military boot, he found himself eternally under the heel of a woman. Perhaps this is not a surprise, however: His wife's eternal "no way" was already hidden in "Norway."

The Eleventh

Emanuel Swedenborg had great admiration for Charles XII, despite the fact that the Swedish king possessed many execrable habits. Thus, for example, while engaging in conversation, Charles would generally grab a button on the clothing of his interlocutor and twist it. Having finished the conversation, Charles would make a quick gesture and one more courtier would leave an audience missing a button. Swedenborg had his buttons sewn on very tightly, and one day Charles said to him with a smile, "I've noticed that you have a very good tailor."

This is a story about a button that was torn off.

According to the third volume of Dahl's famous *Dictionary of the Russian Language,* a button is a "disk or a sphere, a little hat on a peg, which is sewn onto clothing," and he tells us that etymologically the word "button" (in Russian *pugovitsa*) derives from the church Slavic word *pugva* (swelling). I would like to give another explanation for this strange Russian word, which, in my opinion, derives from the verb *pugat'* (to frighten). And the story I will be recounting is truly a scary one.

When the twelfth Charles fled from the battlefield of Poltava in 1709, he found himself in Turkey, where he remained a kind of prisoner for five years. When he returned to Sweden in 1715, Charles again began preparing for war—as was his habit—this time with Norway. The preparations took a long time, for the coffers were empty. Charles ordered the minting of counterfeit money in order to pay for more soldiers, and in 1718 the Swedish army set out on a new campaign. Although general opinion has it otherwise, Charles XII was an extremely enlightened king who spoke three European languages fluently, and his army was also quite polyglot. In addition to Swedes and Finns, there were German and French soldiers, and Charles considered the ideal army to be the Turkish one. With this international composition, the Swedish army laid siege to one of the Norwegian fortresses. One evening, Charles stood, as always, on the breastworks, supervising the military actions. He was reveling in the crackle of gunfire and the whistle of bullets when suddenly his head snapped back and his body went limp. By the time his aides came rushing up to him, it was too late: Charles XII was dead.

Naturally, the siege was raised. His beloved French guards lifted the stretcher carrying the dead body of the Swedish king and carried it off forever to the encyclopedia where it remains to this day under the letter *C*. But, as it happens, another story begins here, for the death of Charles XII marks one of those pages of history in which a mysterious dried flower has been laid. And whenever the book is picked up, it inevitably opens to the page where the dried vegetation is to be found. Let us for a moment become junior Linnaeuses and examine the flower carefully.

The night on which Charles XII died was by no means a particularly martial one. Gunfire crackled and bullets whistled, but they did so more or less out of inertia. It was a dark night; the flashes of gunfire lit the landscape only occasionally, so it is clear that the Norwegians were not actually aiming at the Swedish king. From that time on, rumors flew around the encyclopedia that Charles XII was killed by his own troops—by Swedes—who were tired of his endless wars and who, considering the king's tender age (Charles was only thirty-five), could not figure out how otherwise to put an end to his ruinous bellicosity. But this rumor was countered by the evidence of military investigators: When they examined the mortal wound, no sign of a powder burn, which would have indicated that he had been shot at close range, was discovered. Nor was the bullet found, although it had gone straight through his head.

So the question is, who killed Charles XII? It has been necessary to wait 275 years for an answer to this question, but the most recent excavations on the site of the battlefield have yielded conclusive proof that Charles was indeed killed by his own troops. Here is the story.

Charles XII was not only a warlike and educated king, he was also miserly, even toward himself. Other than his military uniform Charles wore no clothing, and he wore out a uniform per week. In addition to counterfeit money, Charles's mint stamped special buttons for him: They were round, as described in Dahl's dictionary, heavy and a bit elongated, for Charles's uniform was cut from a Turkish pattern. As it happened, Charles was killed on the night after he had put on a new uniform. During the excavations, a number of these special buttons were found in just the spot where the Swedish king generally stood watching the military operations. Why were several buttons found, and what does this mean?

With the help of ballistics testing, criminological induction, and a careful reading of memoirs, it has been possible to piece the following story together. When Charles XII took off his old uniform, someone removed some buttons from it. The found buttons indicate that that someone practiced shooting these Turkish buttons from a gun in order to figure out the distance needed for a successful shot. When the right distance was found, that someone waited for night and, in the complete darkness, shot Charles in the temple, killing him outright. But why did that person decide to kill Charles with his own buttons? The first explanation is the simplest: to avoid the powder burn that is left by a normal bullet and, therefore, to prevent anyone from proving that this was a premeditated killing. But there is another explanation.

There is a Russian proverb that goes "A brave man can't even be killed by a bullet." Charles was indeed brave, and bullets did not find him. According to a different folk belief, you can only kill a werewolf with a silver bullet. But Charles was not a werewolf. The conclusion, therefore, is simple: You can only frighten a brave man to death with a button. Fortunately, however, buttons have changed so much in the past two hundred years that they are no longer dangerous.

The Twelfth

In September 1771 Swedenborg arrived in London. At the dock, he hailed a hansom cab and told the driver to go to his usual London address, the house where he always stayed. Through the window of the cab, on the crowded London streets, Swedenborg happened to see the owner of the house. When Swedenborg called out to him, the man (his name was Shearsmith) came up to Swedenborg and said that he was always happy to see him, but that unfortunately the apartment was occupied by another family for the moment. Nevertheless, Shearsmith hopped into the cab and said that perhaps he would be able to convince the family to take in another lodger, if only for a few days. Having arrived, Shearsmith went upstairs to the family that was occupying Swedenborg's usual apartment, and he soon returned in complete amazement. The tenants, who had never heard of Swedenborg, not only immediately offered to give him a place but, even though they had paid in advance, to move out, this despite the fact that it was very difficult at the time to find a furnished apartment in London. Thus, Swedenborg moved back into Shearsmith's house, and the latter was quite happy. That very night, however, Shearsmith witnessed an extremely strange occurrence. Coming home at one o'clock in the morning and passing by the apartment in which Swedenborg was staying, Shearsmith saw that the door was ajar and that Swedenborg was standing in the doorway between two rooms having an animated conversation with someone, although there was no one in the apartment but Swedenborg himself. And the conversation was strange as well, for it was taking place in a language completely unfamiliar to Shearsmith, although he was a very well educated man. Thus they stood until two or three in the morning: One of them, Swedenborg, was speaking to an invisible person, and the other, Shearsmith, was observing and becoming more and more amazed.

In the morning, Swedenborg came down to breakfast, where he sat down next to another tenant of Shearsmith's. This tenant later told the homeowner about their morning conversation. While drinking his coffee, Swedenborg told the still-sleepy tenant that the night before he had met the apostle Peter, who had come to visit him. "And in general," said Swedenborg, "the apostles frequently visit me."

Then another story occurred the next month; it, too, is documented by contemporaries. While Swedenborg was staying at Shearsmith's, he was visited, as befits a famous countryman, by the Swedish consul in London, one Christopher Springer. After some polite conversation, Swedenborg, who had never met Springer before, began to tell him what his dead friends were doing in the other world. Two particular pieces of information amazed Springer, and he wrote about them in his memoirs. One needs to know that Klas Ekeblad, who had been Springer's most implacable political opponent, had died the previous October. Once Springer and Ekeblad had even fought a duel with swords, but then they had made up, and Ekeblad even tried to buy off his parliamentary opponent. Swedenborg even told Springer the exact sum of the bribe that had been proposed, thus astounding him. According to Swedenborg, "In the other world that secret is a secret no longer." And the second thing was even more incredible. He told Springer that he knew what the Swedish diplomat had been doing nine years earlier—he knew that England had used Springer as its mediator to make peace between Sweden and Prussia. According to Springer, no one other than a very few highly placed and now-dead Englishmen knew anything about this, and so there was no way Swedenborg could have discovered this secret from terrestrial sources unless he was some kind of triple agent. But Swedenborg was no spy. And when Springer asked where he had found all this out, Swedenborg replied, "In the other world."

In December, approximately a month and a half later, Swedenborg had a stroke. He was unconscious for three weeks and could not speak. But after three weeks, Swedenborg suddenly got better and his speech returned. He told his friends and acquaintances (among them Springer) that those were the most frightening weeks of his life, because for a couple of weeks after the stroke he lost his ability to commune with spirits. These are Swedenborg's own words: "It was like a sudden blindness which was accompanied by a crushing depression." But then, while he was still unconscious, everything had come back, and Swedenborg could once again talk to spirits.

The following February, having just read a translation of the latest work of Swedenborg to come out in English, and unaware that Swedenborg was in London, John Wesley, the Protestant leader, wrote in his diary: "Swedenborg is, of course, one of those rare geniuses whom I, and many others, have a tendency to call madmen because he writes only about absurd dreams, incredible fantasies, hopelessly distant from the holy writ and reminiscent of fairy tales." How amazed must Wesley have been when he received a letter containing the following text just a few days later. Here is the text:

> Sir, From the world of spirits I have discovered that you do not agree with me. I would be happy to meet with you if you would be willing to do me the favor of coming to visit. Your obedient servant, Emanuel Swedenborg.

Wesley was flabbergasted (as a number of his friends recalled), and he said to everyone: "How could Swedenborg have even known of my existence, let alone discover my opinion of him, for I have never shared it with anyone. This is indeed a riddle." In any case, Wesley answered Swedenborg that he would be happy to meet with him but that he needed to leave London for six months and therefore asked him to meet at the end of August. Wesley received a reply from Swedenborg in which the latter said that, unfortunately, August would not do because he was intending to leave this world for good on the twenty-ninth of the following month.

Swedenborg told many people that he would die on March 29. One of his regular visitors in London wrote in her diary: "He talks about the date of his death with a smile, as if he were getting married or going on vacation."

On Friday, March 28, 1772, Swedenborg asked a priest to take his confession, and, the entire next day, the predicted one, he worked lying down. He dictated a few letters and wrote a few pages himself. Then he asked what time it was. He was informed that it was 5:00 P.M. He smiled and said to those present: "That is wonderful. Thank you all! May God bless you!" Then he closed his eyes and immediately died.

When he opened his eyes again, he was surrounded by a thick mist, and Swedenborg initially thought that his prediction had not come true and that he was still in this world, in misty London. But the mist did not dissipate, and Swedenborg understood that he had truly died. For, according to Swedenborg, mist, which sounds the same in English and Swedish, is eternal in the other world.

Just like mysticism in this world. No wonder they sound so similar.

Translated by Andrew Wachtel